The Golden Age
of Ironwork

The Golden Age
of Ironwork

text by
Henry Jonas Magaziner
Fellow, American Institute of Architects

photographs by
Robert D. Golding
Fellow, American Society of Photographers

 **SkipJack Press**
Ocean Pines, MD

DEDICATION

In memory of my dear wife

Reba Henken Magaziner

whose influence lives on
in the many who loved her,
the students whose lives she touched,
and the causes she embraced.

Library of Congress Control Number   00-135023
ISBN   1-879535149

Printed in the United States of America
5 4 3 2
First Edition: November 2000

TABLE OF CONTENTS

Introduction

Interest in architectural ironwork has dramatically expanded in recent decades, due in no small part to the pioneering efforts of Margot Gayle, founder of the Friends of Cast Iron Architecture, a national organization devoted to fostering appreciation of iron in architecture, and author of *Cast Iron Architecture in New York* (New York, Dover). 1974. Following the latter publication, similar works for other communities appeared, most notably Robert P. Winthrop's *Cast and Wrought: The Architectural Metalwork of Richmond, Virginia* (Richmond, VA, The Valentine Museum, 1980). In addition, there have been several reprints of ironwork trade catalogues. One of the earliest and most important of these is the 1977 reprint entitled *Victorian Ironwork: A Catalogue* by J. B. Wickersham, sponsored by The Athenæum of Philadelphia with a new introduction by Margot Gayle. But no Philadelphia overview like those for New York City and Richmond has appeared to replace Philip B. Wallace's narrowly-focused *Colonial Ironwork in Old Philadelphia* (New York, 1930).

Now, happily, such a book exists and it is from the hand of an old friend and colleague, Henry Jonas Magaziner, FAIA, who has done far more than update Wallace. He has expanded the coverage well into the twentieth century and added much useful information on the architects, craftsmen, and the buildings of which the ironwork is such an important part. We are fortunate that Henry Magaziner selected as his collaborator the master photographer Robert D. Golding, whose splendid images appear here and in accompanying exhibition at The Athenæum of Philadelphia. The negatives and prints have also been deposited at the Athenæum where they will be available for future reference. We appreciated the support of the William Penn Foundation in making the photography possible and seeing that it became a part of the Athenæum's architectural archive.

It is appropriate that the Athenæum should have a modest involvement in this project. As the principal repository for the records of Philadelphia architecture prior to 1945, the Athenæum has long benefited from the interest and support of Henry Magaziner. As the son of the distinguished Hungarian-born architect Louis Magaziner (1878-1956), whose parents brought him to Philadelphia as a child, and where he attended Central High School and received his architectural degree from the University of Pennsylvania (1900), Henry was destined to follow in his father's steps. The elder Magaziner established his own firm in 1907 and throughout a long career designed many colleges, hospitals, clubs, and banks. Recently his designs for Art Deco motion picture theaters, including the Midtown and Uptown Theaters in Philadelphia, have gained particular recognition. The Athenæum featured several of these in Irvin R. Glazer's *Philadelphia Theaters: A Pictorial Architectural History from the Collection of The Athenæum of Philadelphia* (New York, Dover, 1995), published to accompany the exhibition "Behind the Marquee" at the Athenæum from September 16, 1994 to February 3, 1995. Louis Magaziner's career is one of the best documented for its period in Philadelphia due to the survival of his professional archive at the

Athenæum, a generous gift by his son in the mid-1970s. This archive is catalogued and is found on-line at http://www.PhilaAthenaeum.org/athena.

Henry Jonas Magaziner was born in Philadelphia on September 13, 1911. He attended The University of Pennsylvania where he studied under Paul Cret and received his Bachelor Architecture in 1936. Following graduation he worked in the offices of Day & Zimmermann, Albert Kahn, and in partnership with his father until the latter's death. Through the 1960s he practiced independently until joining the National Park Service in 1972 as Regional Historical Architect and Architectural Historian, Middle Atlantic Region, from which he retired in 1987. Henry continues as a consulting architect specializing in the restoration of historic buildings.

I first met Henry Magaziner and his late wife Reba, whom he married in 1938, through their long association with civic associations in the Germantown, Mt. Airy, and Chestnut Hill neighborhoods. (Reba taught at Germantown Friends School for a quarter century; and for forty years the Magaziners lived in West Mt. Airy, where they raised their two children). Henry appreciates good architecture and design regardless of what period or style happens to be in fashion, and to his trained eye, the Ebenezer Maxwell house (c.1859) seemed an especially significant example of picturesque streetcar villa that so characterized mid-19th-century Germantown. The first efforts to save the Maxwell house by the Germantown Historical Society soon spawned a separate friends group, that ultimately became Ebenezer Maxwell Mansion, Inc., which Henry served as both a board member and President. From the distance of thirty-five years, it is difficult to realize what an effort it required to rally support to purchase a mid-19th century house and open it to the public as a museum. In retrospect, Henry is hailed as a pioneer in the early movement to save significant Victorian buildings in a city besotted with its colonial past and inclined to discount what came thereafter.

All this had already occurred by 1968 when I arrived in Philadelphia. Once I had installed the national office of The Victorian Society in America at the Athenæum, Henry kept nudging me to become involved with and be a supporter of Maxwell Mansion. When the history of that preservation effort is written, Henry's role will loom large. Like many Philadelphians before and since, I learned it was difficult to resist his persistent advocacy or to avoid becoming a devoted friend. Even in "retirement," having reached a stage in life when most individuals would long ago have hung up their spurs and rested on their laurels, Henry launched into *The Golden Age of Ironwork*, which required him to cris-cross the city in blistering summer heat and bitter winter cold to stand shoulder to shoulder with Bob Golding waiting for "just the right light." Readers of this book for generations to come will benefit from what they have accomplished.

Roger W. Moss

The Athenæum of Philadelphia

Foreword

Iron is a dead metal and it is fun to bring it to life.

Samuel Yellin

It is a cruel, bitter cold, February day. The wind is blowing the hats off those not holding them tightly. People are rushing toward shelter. It is hardly a day for standing motionless on the street. Yet a man from the South, an Atlanta banker visiting downtown Philadelphia on a business trip, stands enthralled by St. Mark's Church, in the 1600 block of Locust Street. Its doorway holds him mesmerized. Passing him, I, an historical architect, stop to ask what captivates him so. With a heavy Southern accent, he remarks: "I've been all over Europe and have seen some beautiful doorways; however, this is one of the most magnificent ones I've ever seen. Just look at those hinges!" (f-1)

"Those hinges" were the work of America's greatest artist-blacksmith, Philadelphia's Samuel Yellin (1885-1940). It was he who wrote: "Although iron is the least expensive of all metals, there is no other material which lends itself to more beautiful treatment. Neither is there a material which can be worked more quickly. But unfortunately there are many who do not understand these facts...."[1]

The work of Yellin and other gifted ironsmiths is the subject of this study. It also includes the creations of some of the foundries, that produced cast iron façades and America's finest ornamental cast ironwork.

Iron ore, one of the earth's most common elements, is found in many parts of the world. Thanks to evolving metallurgy, ferrous materials are now more abundant than any other metal products and offer the most utility. Iron ore has been converted into many products over the ages; iron, in its various forms, has been used to produce suits of armor and shields; spears and cannon; railroad rolling stock and tracks; cooking utensils; tools and machines; ranges and stoves; beams, girders, boilers, radiators, pipes and countless other essentials.

Within the period covered by this work, roughly 1840 to 1930, iron and its later derivative steel were used for many monumental constructions including the Eiffel Tower, the dome on the U. S. Capitol, numerous train sheds, the Brooklyn Bridge, and countless skyscrapers. However, ironwork can be just as spectacular on a smaller scale, and this book is intended to demonstrate the incredible versatility and beauty of scaled-down architectural and ornamental masterpieces. These consist principally of the following: cast iron which has a high carbon content (at least 1.7%, to as much as 4%) and is hard and brittle; while wrought iron which has a low carbon content (between 0.01% and 0.035%) and is hard but tough.

Today true "wrought iron," is no longer made. Carbon steel is its modern replacement and therefore is not addressed in this study.

Doorway to St. Mark's, Protestant Episcopal Church, f-1
1625 Locust Street
Samuel Yellin, Artist-blacksmith
Milton Bennett Medary, FAIA; Architect (1874-1929)

St. Mark's is one of the earliest manifestations of the belief that Anglican "High Church" structures should be Gothic in design. The church is one of the country's finest examples of the English Decorated and Perpendicular Styles. It was built between 1848-51, from designs by architect John Notman (1810-1865). It was added to later. In 1923, the entrance and its railings were redone, working from Medary's design. The craftsmen were Nicola d'Ascenzo (1871-1954), gifted stained glass worker, and Samuel Yellin.[2] Yellin's hinges, so greatly admired by the Atlanta banker, are indeed, masterpieces of wrought iron.

Iron can be worked in many ways. Among them are forging, rolling, drawing, machining, stamping, breaking, punching, drilling, and polishing, and it can also be cast. Since both wrought iron and cast iron were important during the Golden Age, we will look at both. Casting is still one of the recommended systems for producing absolutely identical repetitive ironwork, as is mechanical stamping.

Cast iron is brittle and becomes more brittle and crumbles when heated. In contrast, wrought iron is malleable, and becomes even more so when forged in the fire. The artist craftsman forms wrought iron by scrolling, cutting, splitting, twisting, incising, punching, welding, and banding. If it is thin, he can repoussé it – that is he can beat it out from behind and add final details in front.

While both cast and wrought architectural and ornamental ironwork are found everywhere, certain American cities have inherited especially great examples of them. Among those cities are Boston, MA; New York, Albany, and Troy, NY; Baltimore, MD; Richmond, VA; Charleston, SC; New Orleans, LA; Portland, OR; and Philadelphia, PA – cities on the rise during our Age of Iron.

Since Philadelphia is so rich in its collection of cast iron façades as well as being home to both the nation's foremost ornamental iron foundry and America's greatest wrought iron craftsman, I chose the Philadelphia area to illustrate Iron's Golden Age.

Possibly because of its Quaker background, Philadelphia demands that its architectural ironwork serve a functional as well as a decorative purpose. The functional uses of cast iron façades are self evident. Other good Philadelphia ironwork provides security, utility, privacy, as well as ornament. Many of these attributes are found in balconies, stairways, and fire escapes; railings, fences, and grilles; down to small items such as decorative hinges, foot scrapers, and door knockers. Ornamental ironwork is also used for street furniture and garden objects such as fountains.

In its early days, Philadelphia was the great metropolis, the political and financial center of the colonies and, later, of the new republic. In every age, the centers attracted top talent. That was true in Imperial Rome, Renaissance Florence, and Victorian London. Likewise, early Philadelphia drew the country's most capable designer-builders, architects and artisans, and they left a heritage of fine buildings and superb iron craftsmanship.[3]

Even after the capital moved to Washington, and the financial center left for New York, Philadelphia continued to erect splendid buildings with cast iron façades. In the last half of the nineteenth century and early twentieth, Philadelphia became one of the foremost and most diverse manufacturing centers of the world.[4] Its manufacturers and their bankers made huge fortunes.[5] With strong ties, both nationally and internationally, the city became a center of sophisticated taste, and its more affluent citizens were able to authorize the finest work. They commissioned prestigious structures and landscapes, buildings and gardens which required superb iron craftsmanship.

Philadelphia also developed great schools of architecture and landscape architecture. These institutions drew talented designers to the city to teach and, also in most instances, to practice their professions. Often, too, they brought brilliant students to the city. Many of them remained, thus further enriching the city's pool of talent and examples of their work. To translate their drawings into reality, these designers needed gifted craftsmen, including skilled pattern makers, foundry men, and artist ironworkers.

Philadelphia's location made it the logical site for the production of quality cast iron. During the nineteenth century, the iron industry was centered in Pennsylvania. The Commonwealth's iron ore was first smelted in blast furnaces and then poured into molds, called "pigs." Countless iron pigs were shipped to Philadelphia, remelted in its foundries and poured into molds having the desired cast iron shapes, including cast iron façades and treillage. Numerous Philadelphia foundries became nationally important in this field and contributed greatly to the area's economy. Naturally, the products of the city's iron foundries were incorporated into the buildings of the then fast-growing Philadelphia metropolitan area. Many cast iron façades remain in the Old City Historic District.[6] Furthermore, since the city was a great port, its foundries were easily able to ship many of their beautiful castings to distant points such as New Orleans, Savannah, and Mobile.[7] Many New Orleans citizens occupied buildings graced with Philadelphia-made treillage. Later, when these citizens were laid to rest, their bodies were housed in Philadelphia-made cast iron mausoleums. Meanwhile, in Richmond, Virginia, President Monroe's body was enshrined in a magnificent Gothic cast iron tomb made in Philadelphia.[8] (2-1)

In the 20th century, Philadelphia was the home of the Samuel Yellin forge, America's most celebrated wrought iron workshop. Because of its reputation for superb craftsmanship, Yellin ironwork spread coast to coast, from Washington, DC - the National Cathedral, to Washington State – Seattle's Museum of Asian Art – thirty-nine states in all![9] (f-1, f-9, f-10, 1-1, 1-2, 1-3, 1-5, 1-6, 1-9, 1-10)

In 1930, when Colonial Revival architecture was at its peak, Philip B. Wallace produced *Colonial Ironwork in Old Philadelphia; the Craftsmanship of the Early Days of the Republic.* That work, a handsome picture book, covers the period up to about 1830. However, most of the buildings in the Philadelphia area are of later periods and are thus included here. This study discusses and illustrates the architectural uses of iron in both the buildings and landscapes of the area, primarily during the Greek Revival period, the Victorian age, and the early 20th century. There are also a few examples of contemporary work.

This book can be especially helpful to those involved in historical preservation, since a number of those projects involve ironwork. The survey can guide restorers into using ironwork which is appropriate to their buildings and grounds. This is important for restorers of properties on the *National Register of Historic Places*, either individually or as contributing structures within an historic district.

Restorers applying for Historic Preservation Tax Act benefits must follow the *Secretary of the Interior's Standards for Rehabilitation and Guidelines for Rehabilitating Historic Buildings.* Those standards require historical accuracy. Where historical information is not obtainable, the *Standards* give as an "acceptable option for the replacement feature...a new design that is compatible with the remaining character-defining features of the historic building. The renovation work should always take into account the size, scale, and material of the historic building itself and most importantly, should be clearly differentiated, so that a false historical appearance is not created." (11-10, 11-11)

Besides providing information on the appropriateness of certain ironwork, this book also discusses and illustrates good and bad practice in the design and fabrication of architectural ironwork. In highlighting what is good ironwork from the past, it is hoped that this book will inspire better ironwork today.

Throughout this work, where owners' and architects' names are used in connection with the Philadelphia buildings, they have been checked with the records of the Philadelphia Historical Commission. No title searches were made.

Acknowledgments

The author is grateful to the following who, in one way or another, made this work possible: Jack Andrews, William S. Blades, Campbell Thomas & Company, J. Randall Cotton, Nicholas East, Kenneth Finkel, Betsy Halberstadt, Alice Hemenway, Herman R. Henken, Ann Chandler Howell, Roger W. Moss, Sean O'Donnell, Christopher T. Ray, Richard Tyler, Deborah Widiss, William Penn Foundation, and Clare Yellin.

John Kennedy Mansion, f-2
(Now Kennedy-Supplee Mansion)
Valley Forge National Historical Park
Valley Forge, PA
Architect unknown

This mansion, in the Tuscan Villa style, incorporates an outstanding example of cast iron treillage. It was built in 1852 by John Kennedy, owner of a nearby limestone quarry. Later it became the home of the socially prominent Supplee family. In 1852, various foundries were casting such treillage units. However, since Kennedy was in the building products sphere, one can assume that he knew that Robert Wood's Philadelphia foundry was the national leader in the field and that he went there for his mansion's treillage.[10] Over a century later, Valley Forge National Historical Park was created. Since the mansion was located within the historic encampment site, the Park Service acquired it. Even though it was erected decades after the encampment, the Park Service was required to save the structure, because of its architectural importance. The building was in a semi-ruinous state. In 1987, the Park Service leased it to a group of developers, with proviso that they restore it. They were free to rehabilitate it adaptively. John Milner Associates (1968 –) were the architects for restoring it and converting it into an up-scale restaurant.

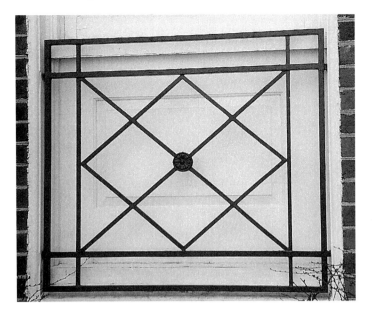

Locust Club, f-3
1614 Locust Street
Levy, Demchick, Supowitz, (1959-1960) Architects

Some architects use purely decorative non-functional ironwork, such as this. However, that is not the Philadelphia tradition. Philadelphians expect ironwork to serve a functional as well as a decorative purpose. The ironwork on this 1960 building gives no support, nor does it protect from intruders, as does a window or door grille. Its strength is not utilized. It faces a fixed, immobile wooden panel. Result: The ironwork seems frivolous and lacking in integrity. (Photograph by author.)

Ethical Society of Philadelphia, f-4, f-5 below
1906-08 Rittenhouse Square
Ralph Bowden Benker (1883-1961), Architect,

In 1929, Benker created the present façade of this c.1850 Italianate structure. Undoubtedly four identical cast iron basement window grilles had been there originally. One had disappeared. Since the pattern of the casting had probably vanished decades ago, a later designer approximated, somewhat freely, the initial design translating it into wrought iron. This affords an interesting contrast between wrought and cast iron. On the one hand, we have the chubby, somewhat opaque original casting. On the other hand we have the more open, springy, wrought iron "copy" shown above it.

Expressing the Strength of Iron, f-6
Stairway in a Philadelphia Townhouse
Magaziner & DiGiorgio (1962-1970), Architects
J. P. Metal Crafts, Ironworkers

Philadelphia tradition dictates that, from an artistic point of view, a strong material such as iron, looks best when its strength is used to maximum advantage. Here the author's use of iron is certainly expressive of the material's strength. The oak treads of the stair, literally hang from the narrow iron pipe railings. (Photograph by Cortlandt V. D. Hubbard)

Short-Favrot House and Fence, f-7, fence detail f-8, facing page
Fourth and Prytania Streets
New Orleans, LA
Henry Howard (1818-1884), Architect

Especially during the 1850's, contractors in New Orleans' famous French Quarter incorporated much ornamental cast iron into their projects. They surrounded the Quarter's buildings with lace-like cast iron treillage, similar to that shown in f-7 and supporting slender cast iron columns. [11] According to Italo Ricciuti, "Cast iron was everywhere, covering the entire faces and much of the sides of buildings…." [12] The popularity of New Orleans' verandahs was not only because of their decorative qualities, they provided pleasant places to sit outdoors, after the sun left them. They also provided cooling shade in the city's sub-tropical climate and allowed windows to remain open during refreshing showers. This was especially important in the days before air conditioning. Many Americans who went down to New Orleans after the Louisiana Purchase, built their homes in what is today called the city's Garden District. These houses, more in the American tradition, were frequently set back within large landscaped lots. Many of them incorporated cast iron treillage and surrounded their grounds with cast iron fences. This particular 1859 fence has an interesting history. According to Margot Gayle, in the 1850's, Dr. Joseph Biamenti ordered a fence using a cornstalk design for his New Orleans home. He wanted to keep his bride "from feeling homesick for her native Iowa." Once the pattern was made, the foundry featured it in its 1858 catalog." [13] Now painted a uniform green, the fence was probably colored in naturalistic hues originally, as were others of its kind. This fence is marked Wood Miltenberger & Co., who were sales representatives of Wood & Perot, of Philadelphia. Quite possibly the ironwork of the verandah was obtained from the same firm. [14]

(The photograph of the Short-Favrot House, above, is from the collections of the Library of Congress.)

Gates to the Childrens Chapel, National Cathedral, f-9
Washington, DC; Samuel Yellin, Artist-blacksmith

This photograph, from the Yellin Archives, was made in Yellin's workshop before the gates were sent to the site. Since these wrought iron gates were for an interior use, and not for security, they were lighter than gates he made for exteriors. The bushes on top provide a particularly light touch.

Gateway within the Museum of Asian Art, f-10
Seattle, Washington; Samuel Yellin, Artist-blacksmith

This photograph is from the Yellin Archives. It was made before the wrought iron gateway was sent on to the site. Yellin loved to create animal heads. Here he fashioned one to be the handle on the bolt.

WROUGHT IRONWORK

Chapter 1

...bars with plain and ornamental twists, spindles and balusters almost as similar as though cast from a single mould, pilasters from 1 to 4 inches wide enriched by carved or applied arabesques, capitals of Corinthian parentage with fanciful details, portraits and panto-mimes in repoussé, luxurious leaves and flowers, bars which divide and, after performing a graceful curve and convolution, rejoin the two parts into a single bar—these are but syllables of the vocabulary which eloquently declaimed the glory of the fifteenth and sixteenth centuries' iron work in Spain.

Gerald K. Geerlings, Wrought Iron in Architecture

While it is true that Samuel Yellin, with his favorite whimsical animal heads in iron, drew more heavily on French Gothic tradition, the Spanish craftsmanship described above could as easily characterize Yellin's prolific output. Unquestionably, he was America's greatest artist-blacksmith.

Yellin was born in Poland, where he learned his craft. He was apprenticed there for ten years, receiving his master's license at age seventeen. Then, after detouring around Europe for four years, he arrived in Philadelphia. It was 1906, and he was twenty-one. Early American craftsmen had fewer mechanical aids at their disposal than their counterparts had in England, so they usually produced simpler designs. However, by Yellin's time, the early twentieth century, all the best devices were available here, and his forge utilized them most creatively. No ironwork challenge was too great for him. His ironwork was as much a fine art as painting or sculpture, so it was most logical for him to have taught at the Pennsylvania Museum and School of Industrial Art (later changed to Philadelphia College of Art and now the University of the Arts).

Yellin's commissions ranged from balconies, railings, grilles, and gates down to lighting fixtures and door hardware. He also produced decorative accessories of every description, ranging from fireplace equipment to candlesticks, signs, and weather vanes.

He described the creation of artistic ironwork in the following way:

"First, draw a sketch to a small scale, so as to obtain the general composition, proportion, silhouette and harmony with the design of surrounding materials or conditions. This sketch should then be developed into full size to obtain details or ornament, various sections and sizes of material, and a general idea of the method of making. At this time careful consideration must be given to the practical use of the piece of work, so that it may serve its purpose in the best manner possible. Workers in iron should always attempt to make everything direct from a drawing, rather than from models. When working from a model, the object becomes more or less a reproduction, whereas the drawings allow a greater opportunity to express the craftsman's individuality.

"Studies or experiments in the actual material are now made, for here many things are revealed which could not possibly be shown on paper. The character of a twisted member or the flexibility of the material might be used for example to show how difficult it would be to conceive many such things in the drawings. For this reason the true craftsman should often make a fragment or portion of the ornament in the actual material first, and make the drawings later."[1]

Contrary to Yellin's admonition, some ironworkers do make their "sketches" in modeling clay. Such studies, in three dimensions, make it easier for them to visualize their finished products.

True wrought iron is almost pure iron, with a minimum of carbon. It has slag, refuse from melting of metal, that varies between 1% and 3% of its contents. The slag is in physical association with the iron and is not alloyed. This gives true wrought iron a laminated, (a layered or fibrous) structure. Softer than cast iron, it is malleable, tough, and resistant to fatigue. It has flowing, sometimes meandering lines, with hammer marks telling of its having been shaped by hand. Depending on how the light hits its component parts, once it has been polished, its color varies from jet black to silver. Interestingly, true wrought iron is quite resistant to rust. It is probably because of this that in England there are still many wrought iron hinges in good condition, dating back to Norman days.[2]

Medieval ironworkers had to hammer out their iron bars from the mass of iron produced by the smelting forges. Today's artist ironworker starts with a bar. To increase its width, he "spreads" it. To lengthen it, he "draws" it by decreasing its cross section. To increase its cross section at a given point, he "upsets" or "shoulders" it.

Now as then, the iron craftsman must plan the entire operation before he thrusts his piece of iron into the forge's fire. There he heats it to an incandesent yellow. He must remove the piece from the flame promptly or the iron will burn, and then he must work it instantly. Because he is shaping iron which is at a yellow heat, he must work it at arms length as dramatic sparks fly in all directions. Gradually the iron changes color from yellow to a dull red. The smith realizes that when he imparts a blow to the top of the piece he must remember that the anvil under it is exerting a force on the opposite face. Thus one wrong blow on top could damage the carefully crafted work he produced previously, now on the bottom. By the time the iron cools and returns to its natural black, it is no longer as responsive to the craftsman and his tools.

The craftsman can hammer, chisel, twist, and beat the piece of heated wrought iron in scores of different ways. He may transform it into spirals; rosettes; trefoils and quatrefoils; happy birds singing love songs to their mates; or snarling, vicious, winged dragons. He converts it into shapes which are muscular and springy. He twists the chubby square or oblong iron bar, transforming it into a piece of sculpture. He bends the bar, producing a pleasing slightly rounded outer corner. In what is called repoussé work, he pounds a thin iron sheet forward from the rear, then puts in the details from the front, producing an embossed figure. (1-4)

To assemble the components of an iron object, the iron craftsman has various options. If he rivets, his rivet heads are not countersunk but remain exposed, becoming part of the design. If he produces a true hand hammered forge weld, he hammers together two pieces of metal which have been brought to a welding heat. Such a weld looks very different from today's acetylene torch or electric weld – it blends perfectly at the point of juncture. If he collars, he combines the parts by strips of iron, bent hot around the abutting members. When the iron cools, the strips, *i.e.*, collars, shrink and clutch the members in a tight grip.

Currently, mild steel is used to fabricate new hand worked metal and to repair old wrought iron members. Strong but easily worked in block or ingot form, it is an alloy of iron which is low in carbon (about 0.10% to 0.20%). Unfortunately, mild steel is not as resistant to corrosion as either true wrought iron or cast iron.

Today stock bars and plates are available in almost any desired dimensions. No work with hammer and anvil is needed to get them to size. However, some fabricators add hammer marks to the metal to make it appear to have been "spread" or "drawn" by hand.

Samuel Yellin addressed this in an article. He writes: "This might be well illustrated in the case of a design composed of horizontal or perpendicular members of one-inch round iron. There should be no attempt to take a one-inch round section and abuse it as described, but instead a one-inch square section should be used, forging it as near to round as the human eye can measure. The bar will then possess the quality of hand wrought craftsmanship and be far superior in character to any disfigured work or, on the other hand, to any machine-like perfection."[3]

Much of today's ironwork involves cold fabrication where the pieces are cut to length, welded together electrically, painted black, and sold by the foot. Shops producing this so-called "ornamental ironwork" make gates, railings, fences and grilles from stock, cast, or stamped elements. Compared to true wrought ironwork, the pieces are usually thin and flimsy with little artistic merit. This is not true wrought ironwork, such as was produced during the Golden Age of Ironwork.

Returning to true wrought ironwork, there are few limitations to the freedom of design of the material. Of course, discrimination should be exercised in applying ironwork to a building. For instance, a beautiful piece of French Renaissance ironwork is inappropriate when applied to a Colonial house. Similarly, a balcony railing is unsuitable when simply applied to a wall without a balcony.

Being a strong material, iron looks best when it is used in a way which takes advantage of its strength, regardless of the design idiom followed. The slight variations in the finished pieces of wrought iron, the deviations between various repetitive features, proclaim that the work is a product of the human hand and not of a mechanical process. The well-crafted piece of true wrought iron is truly a piece of art.

The following examples of Yellin's work at Bryn Mawr College are expressions of his passion for iron and his sensitivity as an artist.

Yellin says: "I love iron. It is the stuff of which the frame of the earth is made. And you can make it say anything you will. It eloquently responds to the hand, at the bidding of the imagination. When I go to rest at night, I can hardly sleep because my mind is aswarm with visions of all the gates and grilles and locks and keys I want to do. I verily believe I shall take my hammer with me when I go to the gate of heaven. If I am denied admission, I shall fashion my own key."[4]

Goodhart Hall Lantern, facing page, 1-2
Bryn Mawr College
Bryn Mawr, PA
Mellor & Meigs (1906-1940),
Architects,[5] Samuel Yellin,
Artist-blacksmith

Goodhart Hall was built in 1928-1929. This Yellin-made lantern is so powerful and animated that it almost seems to move. While it is highly decorative, it is also functional. Its muscularity attests to the strength of iron.

Goodhart Hall, Door Pull, 1-1
Bryn Mawr College, Samuel Yellin, Artist-blacksmith

Yellin's door pulls incorporate the animal-like figures he loved to use. Both the lanterns and the pulls fit in beautifully with the building's Gothic design.

Stair Rail, 1-3
Bryn Mawr College,
Samuel Yellin, Artist-blacksmith

Near Goodhart Hall is this handsome
wrought iron stair rail. Note how
Yellin split some of the balusters, then
twisted them, before extending them
up through the handrail. Finally, he
flattened out the extensions to hold
everything in place.

Bowman Gray Manor, (Graylyn), 1-4
(Now Graylyn Conference Center of Wake Forest University)
Winston-Salem, NC
Luther Lashmit (b. 1899), Architect; J. Barton Benson, (1903-1981) Artist-blacksmith

This huge Norman Revival mansion is eclectic in its interior. It contains an abundance of ironwork, all created by Benson, a Philadelphia artist ironworker who had apprenticed under Yellin. Benson produced it during the years 1927-1929. The pictured detail of an interior gate, complete with stylized portraits of a king and queen, is based on a medieval gate found in Paris. An interesting example of the artist ironworker's craft, its backplate is a fine example of repoussé ironwork.
(Photograph furnished by the Benson family.)

27

Drexel Mansion, 1-5
(Now Curtis Institute of Music)
1724 Locust Street
Peabody and Stearns (1870-1917), Architects
Samuel Yellin, Artist-blacksmith

The Drexels built the important corner mansion at 18th and Locust Streets in 1893. In 1920, they added to it, expanding south on 18th Street. For the expansion, they used the site of the Sibley House. Later, the expanded mansion became the core of the Curtis Institute. Yellin produced both the pictured pieces of ironwork in 1927. For the Locust Street door grilles, he used a floral design. Note how cleverly he used this for the rectangular gates and varied it to adapt it, artistically, to the semi-circular transom.

Drexel Mansion, Addition, 1-6
235 South 18th Street
Horace Wells Sellers
(1857-1933), Architect
Samuel Yellin, Artist-blacksmith

Yellin forged the 18th Street gates for the residence of the Bok family, principal sponsors of the Curtis Institute. Later, the Boks donated the gates to Curtis. Particularly appropriate for a music school, these gates have singing birds atop. Contrast the spirit of these delicate gates with the mood of the gates Yellin produced for the former bank at 15th and Chestnut Streets. (1-10) While floral, the latter gates have a strong, protective mood, most suitable for a bank.

Mennonite Meetinghouse, 1-7
6121 Germantown Avenue
Architect unknown

The Mennonite religious sect originated in the German language area of Switzerland. Renouncing violence and warfare, the first group of Mennonites to arrive in America settled in Germantown in 1683, bringing with them their Germanic culture. They erected a log meetinghouse on this site. Then, in 1770, they replaced it with the present fieldstone building. More recently, the congregation outgrew that meetinghouse, so the historic building now serves as a museum and memorial to the beginnings of the Mennonite sect in North America.[6] The gates to the churchyard are a fine example of the ironworker's art and show their Germanic background. They have much in common with the beautiful 17th century German ironwork shown in Geerling's Wrought Iron in Architecture.[7] The date of the Germantown fence and its gates is unknown. The Mennonites believe it to be mid-19th century. In their archives, the oldest photograph showing the fence is an 1881 print. The fence is so light and graceful that one can almost forget its defensive purpose. It certainly is an artistic embellishment to both the meetinghouse and the street.

F. H. Shelton, House, 1-8
228 South 21st Street
Charles Barton Keen (1868-1931), Architect

In 1902, Keen designed the Georgian Revival façade currently on 228 South 21st Street. Keen's design included this unusually simple and forceful use of iron. His handsome, vigorous front stoop railing demonstrates the strength of the material. Its newel is set back far enough in the stoop to keep the stone from splitting. The top rail is cantilevered out to the edge of the step. The scroll work at the base adds a subtle and sensitive touch.

Yellin's comments would apply to the door below. "When a design is made for a wooden door, it is extremely important in order that the door be completed as one unit, that the trimming be designed in coordination. Very often I receive details of doors and am asked to design hardware. People are disappointed when I write and tell them that that particular door is not suitable for strap hinges, but after receiving a thorough explanation they realize the impossibility of their intentions. Ironwork, particularly, requires background, if it is to count as a decorative feature." [8]

Packard Building Gates, facing page, 1-10
Southeast Corner of 15th and Chestnut Streets
Ritter and Shay (1920-1936), Architects
Samuel Yellin, Artist-blacksmith

These handsome wrought iron gates protected the main banking room of the Pennsylvania Company for Insurance on Lives and the Granting of Annuities. Yellin produced the gates in 1924 – the heaviest that he ever forged and assembled. In the Florentine tradition, they bespeak the strength and security of the bank they were forged to protect. At the same time, they allowed the passer-by to view the bank's handsome interior and the imposing and exceedingly secure-looking vault door. Working from the same Florentine tradition, Yellin also produced the two handsome wrought iron lanterns which flank the gates. In design and scale, these attractive lanterns harmonize admirably with the gates.

Collegiate Chapel of St. Andrew, Philadelphia Divinity School, 1-9
4201 Spruce Street
Zantzinger, Borie and Medary (1910-1929): Architects
Samuel Yellin, Artist-blacksmith

The architects for this complex of buildings were winners of a competition for the commission. Milton B. Medary, Jr., F.A.I.A., was famed for his accomplishments in Gothic Revival work. Here, as in the doorway to St. Mark's Church (f-1), he worked with Yellin, who excelled in Gothic style ironwork. The handsome ironwork on the pictured side door is another example of Yellin's craftsmanship; he produced it in 1925.[9] The ironwork is perfect for such a door. Even if space could be found on a paneled door to position such hinges, they would be out of place.

CAST IRONWORK

Chapter 2

The expressive potential of cast iron is most clearly shown in the extraordinary tomb erected in (Richmond's) Hollywood Cemetery in 1858 to hold the remains of President James Monroe. The tomb ranks as one of the most remarkable achievements in cast iron in the nation. It is in the form of a Gothic reliquary. The medieval reliquary, designed to hold a small relic of a saint, is here expanded to hold an entire sarcophagus. The reliquary is made up of Gothic tracery and is surmounted by an open-work tracery dome. The corners are defined by Gothic pinnacles.(2-1)

Robert P. Winthrop, Cast and Wrought, The Architectural Metalwork of Richmond, Virginia

President Monroe's tomb was indeed a unique artistic and remarkable achievement for the cast iron industry. However, cast iron goes back for many centuries before that tomb. For example, the Philadelphia Museum of Art has an elaborate Korean cast iron tiger, which is about 500 years old.

Nonetheless, cast iron did not become an important building product until the 19th century. In 1824, the invention of the hot blast process in England revolutionized the iron industry. A torrid flame, producing a hotter fire, was created by preheating the combustion air in an adjacent chamber. This technology, coupled with use of coal or coke instead of charcoal, spurred an enormous increase in the quantity of iron which could be cast and cast more cheaply. Parenthetically, since charcoal is made from wood, the change in fuel saved countless trees.

American iron casting followed the English developments rapidly. By the 1840s, cast iron became an important building product here. By 1850, cast iron construction for commercial architecture began in earnest.[1] Its real importance was that it was one of the first manufactured building products which could be produced in impressive quantities. Carved stone had become too expensive, but the Victorian love for ornament was satisfied by the use of cast iron. Endless handsome façades, Palladian, Greek and Roman in concept, issued from the iron foundries. *The Founding of Metals*, by foundryman Edward Kirk (1877), contains this statement: "Iron has come into such general use in modern times that the development of the iron resources of a country may readily indicate the advancement of a nation; for iron has become the symbol of civilization: its value in the arts can be measured only by the progress of the present age, in its adaption to the useful arts; it has kept pace with the scientific discoveries and improvements, so that the uses of iron have become universal; it is worth more to the world than all the other metals combined." [2]

Today molten iron is usually created from scrap. Formerly it was extracted from iron ore. It is an alloy composed primarily of iron and carbon, with varying amounts of silicon, sulfur, manganese and phosphorus. The molten iron flows from the main channel, known as the sow pig, into a series of sand molds arranged somewhat like a nursing litter of pigs. (Hence the name pig iron.) The cooled pigs are shipped to a foundry.

At the foundry, the process used for producing cast iron is as follows:
1. A drawing is made, showing the desired product.
2. A pattern is made of wood. It appears exactly like the ultimate casting.

However, to allow for the shrinkage which will occur as the molten iron cools, the pattern is made slightly larger than the desired casting.

3. In many cases the pattern is mounted to a board, which then defines the parting line of the casting to be produced. See item 6, below.

4. A mold is created by firmly packing sand, with a clay binder, around the pattern. (If mass production is intended, metal molds or flasks are frequently used, because of their durability.)

5. The surface finish sought for the eventual casting is determined by the fineness of the grain of the sand, the metal temperature, compaction/mold hardness, moisture content and clay content.

6. The mold is separated into upper and lower halves.

7. The pattern is removed.

8. The two halves of the mold are reunited, leaving a void where the pattern had been. To prevent separation of the mold halves when iron is introduced into the mold, the two halves may be clamped together, but most often weights are applied.

9. A funnel-shaped access hole, called the sprue, is provided into the top half. It leads to runners which subsequently lead to the void. The main purpose of the sprue is to feed molten metal into the top of a mold.

10. Where there will be a need for entrapped gas to escape from the void, a vent, called a riser, is furnished for that purpose.

11. While the main purpose of any riser opened through the top half of a mold is to feed molten metal to a thich section of a cooling casting, it also allows gases to escape.

12. In either a coke channel furnace or an electric furnace, pig iron is remelted at 2,700 degrees Fahrenheit.

13. A huge ladle, filled with the remelted pig iron is brought to the mold. It is carefully tipped forward to pour its molten iron into the sprue, from which the iron flows into the pattern void.

14. The iron is allowed to cool.

15. After the casting has cooled, it is removed from the mold, cleaned of any clinging sand, and is ground to remove "plus metal," any small amount of iron which has run between the mold halves, as well as any iron left in the sprue or risers.

16. Mounting holes are drilled into the casting.

Occasionally a piece is to remain unfinished on the back. This happens infrequently, because of the roughness and flawed nature of the casting's flat side. However, when this is pre-ferred, steps 6, 8, 9, 10, and 11, above, are omitted. Instead, the molten iron is poured into a one piece mold, laid flat. The iron flows into the void left by the removal of the pattern.

Whether finished on both sides or finished just on the front, cast iron can be machined for assembly. But it is too hard and brittle to be shaped by hammering, rolling or pressing. Large pieces are quite heavy, weighing approximately 430 pounds per cubic foot.

Lamentably, finished castings sometimes contain mold lines, flashing, casting flaws, air holes, cracks, cinders, or cold shuts caused by interrupted pouring or "freezing" of the surface during casting. Also, old cast iron is occasionally found to be excessively brittle.

Regardless of these flaws, New York foundryman Daniel D. Badger (1805-1884) was very positive about cast iron. He claimed that "whatever architectural forms can be carved or wrought in wood or stone, or other materials, can also be faithfully reproduced in iron." While the "cost of highly-wrought beautiful forms in stone and marble, executed with the chisel, is often fatal to their use, they may be executed in iron at a comparatively small outlay, and thus placed within the reach of those who desire to gratify their love of art, or cultivate the public taste."[3]

The iron casting industry became proficient at producing repetitive, elaborate decorative forms such as acanthus leaves, foliated and Vitruvian scrolls, Greek keys, ovals, balls, pineapples, cornucopias, fleur-de-lis, finials, rosettes, and myriad other shapes. On a larger scale, it also produced fences, columns, lintels, and importantly, complete building façades. During the time when cast iron was most widely used, various parts of a finished product were often cast separately and then bolted, pinned, or screwed together. For example, the acanthus leaves used on the capitals of the popular Corinthian columns were usually cast separately and attached to the capitals with screws or pins.

In 1839, Philadelphia architect Thomas Somerville Stewart (1806-1889) used cast iron Corinthian capitals (2-5) for the wooden portico columns fronting the sanctuary at 330 South Thirteenth Street, now known as the Church of St. Luke and the Epiphany. Stewart probably did this to reduce construction costs. Certainly the castings cost the congregation far less than hand carved capitals would have.

Even though wrought and cast iron were used together at times, most wrought iron artist craftsmen disdained decorative cast iron. They felt that mass-produced cast iron was a vulgarization of ironwork, especially since so much early cast iron emulated wrought iron.

Many early cast iron patterns came directly from architectural pattern books showing wrought ironwork. Sometimes even wrought iron collars were imitated in the castings. But these were just imitations, and imitations in any field were, and are, rarely as good as authentic works.

However, cast iron had its own place. When items were designed as artistic castings and not as imitations of wrought iron, they too could become art forms. Castings were particularly cost-effective for elaborate, repetitive decoration. Instead of being muscular and springy, like wrought iron, good cast iron panels were usually plump, quiet, and opaque. They got their decorative character from surface ornament.

There is a certain analogy with furniture design. Furniture connoisseurs rightly prize the great Chippendale style chairs produced by early Philadelphia's Thomas Affleck (d.1795) and William Savery (1721-1788). Of course, those chairs were handmade. However, industrialized America's gifted chair designers of today, people like Charles Eames (b. 1907), create designs for mass production.

So it was with ironwork which was mass produced. Cast iron could not have the subtleties of fine hand-wrought work. Nor could it duplicate the sharp and graceful contours of true wrought iron. While it lacked wrought iron's muscularity and vibrancy, it was far less expensive than hand-wrought work, so it put ironwork within the reach of many people who could never afford to own hand-wrought iron. Starting in the 1850s, even those of modest means could afford elegance by affixing cast iron balconies or porches – like lace embroideries – to the fronts of their homes. They could also add decorative cast iron roof crestings, silhouetting them against the sky. If their houses had gardens, they could install cast iron fountains. They could also station cast iron animals at appropriate garden locations.

Wealthy people could go even further. They could attach cast iron and glass greenhouses to their residences. Without cast iron, it would have been impossible for the 1876 Centennial Exposition in Philadelphia to include the super greenhouse, Horticultural Hall. (2-12)

Many of the decorative cast ironwork features used on houses and gardens all over the country were produced by Philadelphia's progressive Robert Wood (1813-1887) in his Robert Wood foundry (c.1839-1848), then Robert Wood & Co.,Iron & Bronze Foundries. Later the firm became Wood and Perot Iron Foundry (1858-1865) and Wood & Perot Ornamental Iron Works.[4] According to *The Manufactories and Manufacturers of Pennsylvania of the Nineteenth Century*, Philadelphia, (1875). Robert Wood "undertook the manufacture of iron railings, substituting for the stiff patterns, then in use, others of elegant designs, which he found could be produced as cheaply. Reputation was the result, and business increased. More help was engaged, the premises were enlarged, and the infant concern began to prosper.... [Railings] were succeeded by a great variety of other objects in iron, such as vases, garden chairs, arbors, summer houses, fountains, etc...."

Wood believed that "a simple lamp post may be as enduring and useful, as a work of art, as it would be, in its primitive form of a straight unornamented iron tube."

The valuable services of an accomplished designer were secured, and his services retained until his death, when he was succeeded by a sculptor of reputation.... [In 1875] the works gave employment to nearly 300 hands.[5]

Since Pennsylvania was, at that time, the center of iron production, it is not surprising that Philadelphia's foundries were able to become preeminent in producing decorative units. Of course, Wood and Perot's tomb for President Monroe was a unique artistic assignment, but their main business was stock castings. In 1845, this firm issued a large folio engraved catalog. By 1853, the catalog had grown to over three thousand decorative patterns. The thousands of patterns pictured in the Wood catalogs furnished some lesser foundries with models, which they copied unabashedly.[6]

Besides being important as a decorative material, cast iron was important structurally. In 1828, the brilliant Philadelphia architectural genius, William Strickland (1788-1854), utilized cast iron's strength when he recreated the wooden upper portion of Independence Hall's tower. He supported it on four large converging wooden posts, one inside each corner. He rested each post on a cantilevered heavy cast iron shelf plate, inserted into the brickwork below.

Cast iron was good in compression, where it could support about forty tons per square inch, but it was poor in tension. Thus, it was efficient for columns but poor for beams and girders. Before its properties were fully understood, it was used at times for the latter. Sometimes failure resulted. However, the results were more successful when cast iron columns were combined with wrought iron beams.

Throughout the land there are thousands of buildings still being supported by cast iron columns. Many of the columns are not only structural but are also quite decorative. When they are used in interiors, they help to open space. For example, Frank Furness (1839-1912), Philadelphia's gifted Victorian architect, used cast iron both structurally and non-structurally in the University of Pennsylvania's Fisher Fine Arts Library. (2-8)

Philadelphia's famous Academy of Music has its balconies supported by handsome cast iron columns. They were probably cast by H. C. Oram & Company, of the city. While the columns spoil some of the view for persons sitting behind them, it is certainly fortunate that they are slender iron castings and not wide stone piers. (2-4)

President James Monroe's Tomb, 2-1
Hollywood Cemetery
Richmond, Virginia
Albert Lybrock, Designer

No book covering the Golden Age of Ironwork should omit President Monroe's tomb. It was cast in Philadelphia by Wood and Perot. It is described at the head of this chapter of the book. One of the greatest pieces of ironwork ever cast in the United States, it is pictured in Gayle and Look's A Historical Survey of Metals. The accompanying text reads: "Important was the selection of Wood and Perot, manufacturers of ornamental iron, to prepare the patterns, make the molds, and cast the separate parts that would compose this work of art." The words "Robert Wood, Maker" can be found at the edge of the enclosure. In later years, Wood and Perot presented sketches of the tomb on the cover in its sales catalog. It (the tomb) measures 7 feet wide by 10 feet long, with a perforated canopy rising 20 feet to a finial of crockets. Four miniature corner towers enclose side panels filled with Gothic arches and trefoil patterns.[7] Oswald J. Heinrich's original water color rendering of the tomb survives in the collection of the Valentine Museum in Richmond. Both Lybrock, the designer, and Heinrich, the artist, were members of the large German community, which developed in Richmond during the middle of the 19th century.[8] (Photograph from the collections of the Library of Congress)

United States Naval Asylum, 2-2
(Later known as the United States Naval Home)
24th and Grays Ferry Avenue
William Strickland, (1788-1854) Architect

The Naval Home is a National Historic Landmark. It was the nation's first veterans' facility and the original home of the Naval Academy. Biddle Hall, its principal structure, was erected between 1826 and 1833, during the Greek Revival period. As was typical of all of Strickland's work, it was well ahead of most buildings of its period. While his design of the central Greek Ionic portico was probably derived from Stuart and Revett's Antiquities of Athens, his design also embodied cast iron, well before the material came into general use, even in Philadelphia. By his use of cast iron beams supporting brick segmental vaults, and brick "partitions", Strickland attempted to make the building as fireproof as possible. On the two long wings flanking the Classical portico, he built verandas facing the street.[9] They were supported by hollow cast iron columns, eight inches in diameter, designed to harmonize with the portico. The verandahs served both functional and aesthetic purposes. In this period "fresh air" was thought to be medically beneficial. Hence, it was considered important to provide these verandas, where sickly residents could go outside without leaving their floors. Aesthetically, by casting deep shadows, the verandas kept the building from appearing ponderous and boring. The contrast between the masonry piers on the first floor and the slender cast iron columns above them is expressive of the strength of cast iron, when used in compression. Currently deserted, the building is to become a part of a residential development.

Philadelphia's City Hall, 2-3
Broad and Market Streets
John McArthur, Jr. (1823-1890), Architect

The architecture of City Hall was strongly influenced by the architecture of the Napoleon III additions to the Louvre, in Paris. While City Hall was still on the drawing boards in June, 1874, architect John McArthur, appointed Thomas Ustick Walter (1804-1887) as his "Assistant." Michael J. Lewis, who surveyed Walter's diaries, preserved at the Athenaeum, states that one of Walter's last assignments appears to have been the preparation of the tower's construction details. Walter was convinced of cast iron's great potential. He had been the architect for the cast iron dome on the United States capitol in Washington; therefore, his experience in Washington is probably what led him to design the upper portion of City Hall's tower in cast iron. The tower concept was heightened from the earlier design. This was made possible by choosing cast iron for the upper portion, a far lighter material than the originally proposed masonry. The cast iron plates lasted there for over a century but were replaced recently. This was because "rust and material disintegration [including fractures] had occurred especially along the edges and at penetrations [bolt holes]," "and the pins [bolts] securing the plates had rusted badly."[10] Nevertheless, many cast iron decorative features remain on the building. Among them are the cast iron embellishments which outline the various planes of the mansards.

Academy of Music, 2-4
Broad and Locust Streets
LeBrun and Runge (1855-1857), Architects

When it opened in 1857, the Academy was state of the art acoustically. So was its engineering, which employed much cast iron. The columns used to support the balconies are cast iron. The architects decided to turn these functional necessities into decorative features. Hence the beautifully embellished column capitals. Gilding them made them even more decorative.

Church of St. Luke, 2-5
(Now the Church of St. Luke and the Epiphany)
330 South 13th Street
Thomas S. Stewart, Architect

Stewart became architect for this church as a result of winning a competition. It was built in 1839-1840 and is an excellent example of Greek Revival architecture. Typical of many such churches, it has a classical portico. The columns forming the portico are "fluted [wood] columns, with cast iron bases and Corinthian caps."[11] Since the entire columns are painted, the use of different materials is not evident. Certainly Stewart saved the congregation money in not requiring the column bases to be turned and the elaborate Corinthian capitals to be carved. Stewart also used cast iron within the church and for the handsome cast iron fence. Note how the fence incorporates Grecian decorative elements.

Helen Orne Clark Dennison House, 2-6
231 South 42nd Street
Architect unknown

This house is part of a development by John D. Jones, speculative building on a grand scale. Its first owner, Mrs. Dennison, was the daughter of E. W. Clark, a wealthy banker. In 1865, when this house was built, the area was suburban. The suburbs had become accessible by trolley car lines and commuter railroads. Suburban families wanted to get away from the polluted air of the industrial city and move "back to nature." At the same time, they wanted people to know that they were not country yokels but sophisticated city people. This fence symbolizes all the above, eloquently. It combines a naturalistic luxuriant rinceau design, rendered with grapevines, above a cultured, disciplined, geometric Greek key base. The fence is a dramatic example of the richness which could be achieved by the use of cast iron.

Second Bank of the United States, 2-7
Library Street, west of 4th Street
(Independence National Historical Park)
William Strickland, Architect

A Greek Revival structure, the Second Bank was America's first public building based on the design of the Parthenon in Athens. It was built between 1818 and 1824, in the age of architectural symbolism, when the young republic considered itself to be the reborn Greek democracy. This fence is a perfect example of a symbolic object. The dignified, sedate design is quite protective and is certainly most suitable for a bank. Consistent with the stately Greek Doric architecture of the building, the fence employs the Classical Greek anthemion pattern.[12] The defensive spearheads suggest to the public that the treasures within are safeguarded. To potential intruders they say "Keep out!" Being so massive, the fence was perfect for casting and would have been difficult to produce in wrought iron.

Anne & Jerome Fisher Fine Arts Library, 2-8
University of Pennsylvania
34th Street below Walnut
Furness, Evans and Co. (1886-1928), Architects

Frequently called the "Furness Library," this structure was built in 1888-1889. When Furness designed it, cast iron was being used extensively. He used it for non-structural purposes such as the supporting columns and the lace-like brackets that keep them in a correct vertical position. The latter embody a design feature which Furness was fond, a curve reminiscent of Gothic arches. Whenever he used cast iron, he took advantage of its decorative possibilities.[13] The balustrade panels are wrought iron, making a wonderful combination of cast and wrought iron.

Masonic Temple, 2-9
1 North Broad Street
James H. Windrim, F.A.I.A. (1840-1919), Architect

This Norman Style structure was erected between 1868 and 1873. It houses dramatic meeting rooms of various architectural revivals – among them Egyptian, Ionic, Gothic, to name just a few. The building is also a treasure trove of beautiful ironwork. The sensational two main stairways are certainly among the most spectacular examples in the city, of the iron founders art. They bear the following inscription repeatedly, "Robert Wood & Co. Makers. Phila." They have concealed wrought iron beams for support. The front stairway has granite treads placed on the castings. Granite is omitted on the pictured rear stairway. Excepting for its mahogany handrail, it is entirely a series of remarkable castings.
(Thanks are due the Grand Lodge of Free and Accepted Masons of Pennsylvania for allowing this photograph to be taken.)

Sixth National Bank, 2-10
(Now a First Union Bank branch)
201 Pine Street, Architect unknown

The design of this 1868 bank was derived from the 1533 Loggia Consiglio, a Renaissance structure in Padua, Italy. What stands today was original- ly the cast iron first floor façade of a three story building. The missing upper floors had brick walls. The castings came from the Philadelphia foundry of H. C. Oram & Co. In 1968, George B. Roberts (1900-1975), architect for the previous owner, inserted the current Pine Street entrance. He did it with sensitivity, not interrupting the regular rhythm of the arches.

133 Arch Street, 2-11
Architect unknown

The first floor façade of this building is cast iron. Above that, the walls are of conventional masonry construction, with one exception, the lintels are cast iron. The cast iron lintels had several advantages: Unlike wooden lintels, they were less likely to rot. They were more economical than brick arches, such as are on the adjoining building at 135 Arch Street. They could easily take various shapes, even arched shapes, such as these. They could be cast with surface decoration, as pictured here. That was substantially cheaper than cutting the decoration on each stone lintel would have been. (Undoubtedly the pictured building was more handsome before the unsightly exterior fire escape was added.)

GARTENBAU AUSSTELL⁵ GEB. HORTICULTURAL HALL GALERIE D'HORTICULTURE.

CENTENNIAL INTERNATIONAL EXHIBITION.
1876.

Horticultural Hall, 2-12
One of the major structures within the Centennial International Exhibition, Philadelphia, 1876
Hermann J. Schwarzmann (1846-1891), Architect

Horticultural Hall typified the period's interest in new materials and methods of construction. It was certainly an outstanding example of nineteenth century American architecture. In his use of glass and cast iron, Schwarzmann recalled the Crystal Palace, which Sir Joseph Paxton (c.1802-1865) had designed for the London Exhibition of twenty-five years before. Unfortunately, Horticultural Hall was demolished in 1955.
(Picture from the archives of the Library Company of Philadelphia)

Advertisement for Robert Wood's Steam Iron Railing Manufactory, 2-13, facing page
Ridge Road above Buttonwood Street, Philadelphia

Elizabeth M. Geffen tells us: Robert Wood's firm became famous all over the United States for its ornamental cast iron, at the height of its popularity in the 1850s. [It was] used for "the adornment of dwelling-places, breathing-places, and last resting-places" of Americans: Much of Wood's ironwork still ornaments New Orleans, Savannah, and Mobile. Pig iron was sent to Philadelphia, where it was remelted and cast into decorative shapes. Then it was sent to the South by ship. Undoubtedly it was because of Wood's leadership in the field that the firm was selected to cast President Monroe's tomb in Richmond. (2-1) Many of the names of specific foundries, original owners, architects, builders, and years of erection come from Ralph Chiumenti's definitive research. He states that his study "is based largely upon accounts in period newspapers." His study and resulting 1976 pamphlet, Cast Iron Architecture in Philadelphia, were commissioned jointely by the Friends of Cast Iron Architecture and the Old City Civic Association of Philadelphia. Lamentley not all of the buildings mentioned in Chiumenti's 1976 study are still standing. The analyses are the author's. (Advertisement from the archives of the Library Company of Philadelphia)

CAST IRON FAÇADES

Chapter 3

Let any citizen imagine the benefits that would be conferred upon the public by sub-stituting cast iron buildings for those of brick....There would appear the space for the building, and all clean and quiet around it Monday morning. In a few moments some carts would arrive with beautiful cast iron blocks, and a few men with derrick, block and tackle, would be quietly hoisting these blocks and fitting them into their places, and per-haps by evening – in a few days at most – a building, which would endure for ages, will be standing erect, in dignity and beauty....

Public Ledger, Philadelphia, July 13, 1852

As early as 1828-1829, Philadelphia architect John Haviland (1792-1852) designed the front of the Miners' Bank in Pottsville, Pennsylvania, facing its masonry structure with iron plates, grooved to imitate rusticated stone. Then he painted it to look like cut stone,[1] Also, as cited above, in 1833 avant garde architect William Strickland used cast iron columns for the verandas on the now vacant and sadly neglected Biddle Hall at the U.S. Naval Asylum, later known as the Naval Home. (2-2)

Although cast iron façades had been built in Constantinople, Turkey, as early as 1833, the full cast iron façade had yet to appear in America. However, in 1848, James Bogardus (1800-1874) produced one. He did this when – in three days – he erected the five story cast iron façade for John Milhau's drugstore in New York. Then, shortly after that, and using the same molds for the façade, he built the Laing Stores in New York, complet-ing the façade in two months. Next he cast the façades for his own factory.[2]

In a self-laudatory 1858 sales essay, he wrote: "...Mr. Bogardus's present factory, is of five stories, and was designed to be a model of its kind. Since its erection, it has not been difficult to convince anyone who will take the trouble to examine it, that SUCH BUILDINGS COMBINE UNEQUALED ADVANTAGES OF ORNAMENT, STRENGTH, DURABILITY, AND ECON-OMY: WHILST THEY ARE AT THE SAME TIME, ABSOLUTELY SECURE AGAINST DANGER FROM FIRE, LIGHTNING, AND AN IMPERFECT FOUNDATION."[3]

He had started a trend.

Bogardus was a self-taught architect-engineer. His multistory self-sup-porting cast iron façades were among the first such in the country and one of the earliest applications of prefabrication to American architecture. In extolling the virtues of his product, Bogardus wrote: "Such a building may be erected with extraordinary facility, and at all seasons of the year. No plumb is needed, no square, no level. As fast as the pieces can be handled, they may be adjusted and secured by the most ignorant workman; the build-ing cannot fail to be perpendicular and firm. And if, for some reason, the client was not satisfied, the cast iron pile could always be carted away. It follows that, a building once erected, it may be taken to pieces with the same facility and dispatch."

The ease of the erection (or disassembly) of cast iron façades was not the only reason they became so popular for the commercial areas of our cities. An architectural magazine of the time contains this comment: "There is one very desirable object to be attained by the use of iron as the material for architectural fronts of stores. We allude to the perfect admission of light. When a whole building is devoted to business purposes, such as showrooms, or working rooms over the store, it is an immense advantage to get rid of the obstruction of brick, or stone, which so tend to darken the different stories, and the weight of which, on the light fragile store-front on which they bear, is so unpleasing to the eye, as well as conducive to danger to the building."[4]

Beyond daylight, they appealed to architects for many additional reasons:

* Their walls were much thinner and lighter than masonry.

* They were readily expandable; their forms could be repeated to either lengthen or heighten a building, as desired.

* They lent themselves easily for building modernization.

* When former residential buildings were retooled for commercial uses, new cast iron fronts could be quickly applied.

* The slender cast iron columns or piers on the ground floor façades permitted larger expanses of glass show windows, thus allowing for larger displays of merchandise.

* Slim as they were, such columns could nevertheless support the weight of the façades of the upper floors, even when they were of heavy masonry.

* Importantly, at the time of their greatest popularity, which lasted into the late 1880s, according to Bogardus, cast iron façades were supposed to be "perfectly fireproof."

Early America had experienced some disastrous fires, so architects and builders undertook to make buildings more fire resistant. Alexander Parris (1780-1852), the gifted Boston architect, attempted to solve this problem in an unusual way. For the Boston Navy Yard, he designed a building with granite interior piers. Between the piers, he used granite girders supporting the floor system.

Some Philadelphia architects resorted to granite columns and lintels to create commercial first floor façades. They utilized the great strength of granite to keep structural elements at a minimum on the ground floor and provide maximum show-window width. A number of such façades can be seen on Front Street, in Philadelphia's Old City Historic District. However, by 1850 other talented architects followed Bogardus's lead and resorted to cast iron as a far cheaper attempt at fireproof construction.[5]

While iron had been available for centuries, its use in buildings had been restricted to nails, screws, bolts, tie rods, and hardware. Until the middle of the 19th century, it was not available in large, economical quantities.[6] Then it began to appear in bridges, water towers, and greenhouses. Once iron became available in economical quantities, full cast iron façades became possible. Among the Philadelphia foundries which produced such iron fronts, were the Cresswell foundries; Deveny & Hitzeroth; Reeves, Buck & Co.; J. A. Gendell; J. S. Field & Co.; and H. C. Oram & Company. In 1871, another Philadelphia firm, Royer Brothers' Builders' Iron Foundry, produced the cast iron for the Grand Opera House in

Wilmington, Delaware.[7] Philadelphia cast iron fronts were also shipped to distant points. The catalog of the Philadelphia Architectural Iron Company mentions its important façades in New Orleans.[8]

To construct such façades, conventional masonry foundations were first built. Holes were introduced into their top faces and wrought iron bolts were inserted. The lowest cast iron units were fitted over the upper halves of the bolts. Then higher cast iron units were attached to the lower ones, again using bolts. While some of the buildings incorporated cast iron interior columns, most of the structures behind the cast iron fronts were of conventional construction, with brick walls, wooden joists and floors.

The cast iron fronts were often elaborate, combining architecture, engineering, fine arts and advertising. Over the show windows there were decorative lintels or arches of iron, sometimes bearing the names of the owners, the type of merchandise they sold, and the addresses or dates of the buildings. Often the ironwork had the "signature" of the foundries cast into the column bases. Typical "signatures" can be seen on the fronts of 309-311 and 718 Arch Street.

When the cast iron was carried up the entire fronts, the buildings would usually be capped with elaborate, highly sculptured cornices.[9] However, after the 1850s, many of the cornice assemblies were sheet metal, typically zinc. In all cases, the fronts of the castings were painted, not just to prevent rust but, typically, to make the buildings look like stone. When the iron surfaces were smooth, sand was frequently mixed with the paint to give the castings a stone-like texture. When the castings themselves had a stone-like texture, which would show through the paint, sand was unnecessary.

While the exposed surfaces of cast iron were protected by paint, their uncoated backs were allowed to oxidize. Since Philadelphia's relative humidity often reached 65% or higher, oxidation occurred rapidly. Moisture got to the backs through the joints. Rust started as light warm tans, then gradually became chocolate browns. The oxidized iron actually became a protective coating.[10]

The use of cast iron enabled architects to create far more decorative buildings and to do so economically. Consequently, it had many strong defenders among sophisticated critics, who argued that decorative cast iron would educate the public in the arts. However, numerous other cultured Americans had a different view – a view influenced by the widely read English architectural philosopher John Ruskin. In his *Seven Lamps of Architecture*, Ruskin did "not admit iron as a constructive material." Nevertheless, he prophesied that "the time is probably near when a new system of architectural laws will be developed, adapted entirely to metallic construction."

Although hundreds of buildings in the older sections of our cities retain their exterior or interior cast iron columns, such as shown on 10-12, cast iron façades gradually went out of favor. Among the factors that caused this to happen were:

* Rusting occurred on the wrought iron bolts, which held everything together. As a result, a number of 19th century façades and fountains failed.

* Galvanized sheet metal appeared. It is a low carbon metal plated with

zinc. Lead and tin are trace metals in the plating. It could be stamped in a number of patterns, cut, bent and soldered. Far lighter than cast iron, it could be used for cornices, for decorative lintels, and for covering the faces of projecting frame bay windows.

    * Another material appeared, which was capable of reproducing elaborate decoration more cheaply than cast iron. That was terra cotta, which remained popular until about 1920. Terra cotta is clay which, after being shaped mechanically, is fired and then glazed. The glaze sheathes, colors, and protects the body within. The famous 1913 Woolworth Building, in New York, is sheathed in this material.

    * About 1856, the Bessemer converter was developed.[11] It could transform twenty tons of pig iron into steel in ten minutes. Unlike cast iron, steel was strong in tension as well as compression.

    * A few years later, another advance occurred. Sir William Siemens invented the open-hearth process for making steel.

    * Then, in 1883-85, architect-engineer William LeBaron Jenney (1832-1907) designed Chicago's Home Insurance Building. He used Bessemer steel beams and skeletal steel construction on the upper floors.[12] From then on, steel replaced cast iron for structural purposes.

    * Finally, in 1904, a disastrous fire completely destroyed Baltimore's cast iron Sun Building. Bogardus notwithstanding, this proved that cast iron structures were anything but "perfectly fireproof."[13]

The day of the cast iron façade was over.

The 1900-01 façade of 56-60 North 2nd Street, Philadelphia, was one of the last cast iron fronts to be erected in the country. (3-9) Although cast iron façades were no longer erected, they had played an important role in architectural evolution. The nineteenth century's utilization of cast iron, and later steel, as the basic structural system of buildings, has proven to be one of the pivotal steps in the history of the world's architecture.

Even though cast iron construction had various defects, it foretold modern steel skeletal construction. Without that type of construction, today's skyscraper would never have developed. Iron framed exterior walls, in part assemblies of prefabricated elements were the forerunners of today's curtain wall units. Sadly, with the urban renewal of the 1950s and the cutting of highways through the older sections of American cities, hundreds of these cast iron façades have disappeared. Thus the nation has lost much important evidence of the evolutionary process, which produced today's buildings.

Smythe Stores, 3-1, facing page
103-111 Arch Street
Architect unknown

Erected in 1855-57, by Samuel Smythe, this group of façade castings is attributed to H. C. Oram. It has undergone many changes: in 1913, the unit at 107 Arch Street was removed to enable trolley cars to loop around the buildings and return uptown. With the trolleys now gone, the "missing tooth" was restored with exact fiberglass reproductions of the original cast iron. When I-95 was put through, 101 Arch Street, the most easterly unit, was demolished so as to allow Front Street to be relocated.[14] The assemblage is currently fifteen bays wide, as expressed by columns on the façade. It has the longest street frontage of any cast iron construction in Philadelphia. Internally, it is divided by party walls. While originally built to have stores on the first floor, today the entire complex has been converted into condominium apartments. These five story cast iron façades present an interesting and free interpretation of Venetian Renaissance architecture. The first floor has a continuous cornice on acanthus modillions. The next three floors each have entablatures, which break above the engaged main columns. Originally, the buildings had "a full entablature at the eaves" with a dentil and modillion cornice. That was removed after 1920. Also the columns' Corinthian capital drums had acanthus leaves.[15] Typically, the attaching members failed, and the leaves were lost. The floor heights diminish as they ascend. This saved construction costs and makes the assemblage appear to be taller than it actually is.

Fox and Ingersoll Partnership, 3-2
54-58 North Third Street, Architect unknown

This building was probably erected in 1851. D. R. Knight's insurance survey of that year indicates that the cast iron façade's "Lower story has....iron piers & lintels, & four large brackets supporting a Balcony with a Fancy Iron railing....The second story...[has] two clustered columns with moulded caps supporting an Entablature also of Iron...." A 1905 insurance survey indicates that these buildings were a "Hotel, in common with 60 North 3rd Street."[16] The front of 54 North Third Street is unusual in several ways. While many cast iron façades have brick starting on the second floor, this brickwork starts on the third. The first floor ironwork mixes Classical acanthus leaves with Gothic arch-faced columns. However, the second floor detailing is purely Gothic.

St. Charles Hotel, 3-3
60-66 North Third Street
Architect unknown

Erected in 1851 by Charles A. Rubicam, this is the nation's oldest remaining iron façade.[17] The building has an interesting history. A newspaper account of March 13, 1851, says: "The first and second stories of the fronts of the stores are to be granite, with neat cluster columns, and the three upper stories of Connecticut brown stone." Possibly, the prices for masonry came in too high, or Rubicam felt that he could save time by changing to cast iron. In any event, by April 25, 1851, the newspaper stated that: [The former building on the site] "is to be razed to the ground, in order to erect a large five story hotel with an iron front.... The cast iron front will greatly improve the vicinity in which it is to be put up....There can be no material that is better calculated for fronts of buildings than Pennsylvania iron, and certainly nothing is more durable." By October 30, 1851, the front was apparently up. The newspaper stated that the front is "painted and sanded so as to resemble brown stone."[18] By 1973 the former hotel was owned by the Philadelphia Yearly Meeting of the Society of Friends. They intended to demolish it, to create a parking area for their adjoining meetinghouse. Fortunately, they had a change of heart. Now retrofitted into apartments on the upper floors, the first floor has shops, as it did originally. The entire façade is cast iron. Originally, it had a "Balcony at the second story supported with 10 iron brackets with a fancy iron railing around 10 Iron posts and lintels in the lower story."[19] The upper floors are "iron ashlar," which clearly illustrates the designer's attempt to make the structure appear to be masonry. Its interior columns are also cast iron. While the building is Italianate in style, the antefixes and other features above some of the windows have Grecian origins. Typical of the cast iron façades, it has slender cast iron columns at the street level. The columns are similar to those of the adjoining building.

309-11 Arch Street, 3-4
Architect unknown

The cast iron columns on this front bear the mark of the Samuel J. Cresswell Foundry in Philadelphia. Above them, the building provides an attractive example of the bricklayer's craft. The piers are decorated with terra cotta features. Since the embellished terra cotta lintel units have no structural strength, they undoubtedly house iron lintels. The contrast of the slim cast iron columns, versus the heavier brick piers above, attest to the strength of the cast iron.

Strawberry Court, 3-5
14-18 South Strawberry Street
Architect unknown

This 1850's façade exemplifies a frequent use of cast iron. The first floor front, originally shops, is cast iron. The upper floors are of conventional brick construction, which was cheaper. The relatively narrow cast iron columns permitted maximum width shop front openings between them. Note how much more glass area there is on the first floor, as opposed to the glass area in the masonry above. Unlike so many other remaining cast iron columns, these with their modified Corinthian capitals, are complete. When a façade easement was established for this property, all loose cast iron parts had to be reanchored.[20] The first floor cast iron has the signature of Daniel D. Badger's firm, the Architectural Iron Works of New York.

**Harris Steam Power
Printing House, 3-6**
*(Later part of Lit Brothers Department
Store. Now: "The Cast Iron Building")
718 Arch Street
Architect unknown*

*The façades of 719-21 Market Street are
cast iron. Most Market Street façades of the
former Lit Brothers' building complex are of
other materials. However, 718 Arch Street
has its entire façade of cast iron. This building and the Smythe Stores have the two
largest cast iron façades remaining in the
city. The castings at 718 Arch Street are
signed by Philadelphia's Deveney &
Hitzeroth. Hitzeroth was in the foundry
business from 1871 to 1895 but Deveny
and Hitzeroth existed in 1880 only. The
façade design of the Harris printing plant
was influenced by North Italian architectural traditions. Its first floor piers and
colonettes support all the other floors. The
latter have semi-elliptical arched openings
with 2/2 sash. While the design of the window surrounds remains constant, floor
heights diminish as the building ascends. As
with the Smythe Stores, the diminishing floor
heights here not only reduced construction
costs but were conceived to make the structure appear taller than it actually was. It
was five stories in 1887. However, by 1896
two more floors had been added.[21] In 1982,
the building was slated for demolition but it
was saved and converted into offices.*

Hope Engine Company No.17, 3-7
(Now the Ray K. Metzker studio and residence)
733-735 South 6th Street
Hoxie and Button (1849-1851), Architects

This quaint little former firehouse is far taller than the neighboring buildings. The height was required for hanging fire hoses to dry. It was built in 1851-2 to house a volunteer fire company and served as a firehouse until 1871. Later, from 1871 to 1920, it was the home of a fraternal lodge.[22] Now it has undergone yet another change of life. The building's Italianate design, with Romanesque detailing, is similar to that found in pattern books of the period, especially those by Samuel Sloan (1815-1884).[23] The façade is not all cast iron. However, excepting for the cornice, all decorative features plus the arches over the openings and the engaged columns, with their composite-ordered capitals, are of that material. The balance of the façade is stuccoed brick, which was originally coated with sanded paint to resemble stone. To save the expense of building a masonry arch, the architects used cast iron to create the wide fire engine doorway. Then they transferred the weight of the tall superstructure to the slender cast iron columns. All original castings were by William Trout & Co. of Chester, PA. The cornice was wood, its central feature being a carved fire hose nozzle. In 1976, the current owner restored the building and had new castings made to replace all castings then missing. He retained the wooden carved fire hose nozzle but replaced the balance of the original wooden cornice with a fiberglass replica.[24] Then he repainted the building colorfully and most attractively.

***Store of Edgar A. Miller & Co.,
3-8***
45 North 2nd Street
*John Riddell (1814-c.1871),
Architect*

With its two story pilaster base surmounted by three story pilasters, all Corinthian, and capped with a bracketed metal cornice, this five-story Italianate cast iron front was one of four similar ones built in 1852 from Riddell's designs. The other three were 35 South 3rd Street, 61-63 North 3rd Street, and 16 Bank Street. Here, on 2nd Street, one also finds "iron ashlar," i. e., ironwork imitating ashlar stonework. In all likelihood, the original paint on the ironwork had a sand admixture in it to create the impression of stone. All were probably cast by the Tiffany & Bottom Ironworks, of Trenton, NJ.[25]

Tuttleman Brothers & Faggen Building, 3-9
56-60 North 2nd Street
Thomas Stephen (1863-1953), Architect

These three brick structures, originally four stories high, were built by Alfred W. Adolph & Eli Keen in 1861. In 1900-01, Camden architect Stephen added a floor, modernized the buildings, and refaced them with cast iron. Formerly a factory, they are now apartments with stores at the street level.[26] This is one of the nation's last cast iron fronts. It shows the influence of the Chicago school of architecture, where a series of seminal buildings developed today's skeletal frame structure. While Stephen applied some Queen Anne detailing to his castings, the front he designed bears a resemblance to Chicago's notable Ayer Building, built in 1900. Its architects were Holabird and Roche.[27] Similar to today's skeleton steel construction, Stephen's front suggests ferrous post and beam construction. It makes no pretense of being stone. Most of the front is glass, with vertical supports being kept to a minimum.

FENCES AND RAILINGS

Chapter 4

Monuments are not infrequently surrounded with iron railings, in the details of which the characteristics of the style of architecture which prevailed at the point of their erection are to be detected.

John Henry Parker, Classic Dictionary of Architecture, 1875.

While the author of the above was a British subject commenting on the 1875 British scene, he could just as well have been writing about the 1875 American scene.

Although fences are generally utilitarian elements today, in Victorian America, fences were considered important features in a site's overall design. Accordingly, most capable architects of the time either designed their fences or selected them from catalogs or architectural pattern books. In his building pattern book, prominent Philadelphia architect Samuel Sloan briefly discussed which designs were suitable for different types of homes: "None of the appendages to a country seat, better repays an expenditure of taste and money than the fencing. Whatever the size of the grounds attached, the enclosure is an important feature in the landscape.... It may be of stone, brick, iron or wood. The two latter admitting a greater variety of pattern, are more suitable than a wall of either stone or brick."[1]

Cast iron certainly admitted a "greater variety of pattern." It was capable of pictorial expression to a degree which no other type of fencing had ever approximated. Such fences lent themselves readily to reflecting the architectural styles of the buildings they surrounded. For example, it was now possible for the designer of a Gothic Revival house to enclose its front lawn with a cast iron fence rendition of Gothic tracery, combining this with a Gothic rose window gate.[2] Gothic tracery fences were particularly popular for church grounds and cemetery plots. While modern cemetery managers tend to discourage fences surrounding family burial plots, during the Victorian period, fences defining such burial plots were quite popular. Furthermore, since this was a period of architectural symbolism, cemetery fence designs frequently incorporated not only tokens of religion, but also of mourning. (4-3)

Returning to the land of the living, in rural America fences were most often erected to keep animals, such as horses, cows, sheep, and pigs, away from the house. However, in urban areas, fences were more frequently installed to keep the animals in. Those animals were usually dogs. Some fences were friendly reminders of the location of the property line. Others were aggressively defensive. One of the most popular defensive designs was composite fencing, marrying cast spearheads to wrought iron fence rods. With such a fence, Roman fasces were often used as gate posts, alluding to the use of military force against the unwelcome visitor. Characteristically, from 1811 until the 1870s, Independence Square had "iron palisades" around the square.[3]

Picturesque fence designs were also developed for specific needs. For example, Wood and Perot even produced the cast iron cornstalk fence pictured in photographs.[4] (f-7, f-8)

From a purely practical point of view, the traditional white wooden picket fences lost out to cast iron. Iron fences lasted longer and offered endless possibilities of design. An 1859 advertisement by Wood, Miltenberger & Co., New Orleans branch office of Wood & Perot, stated that "200 varieties of Gallery Railings" and "50 [patterns] for verandahs" were available.[5] Patterns were frequently mixed and the same cast iron elements were combined in different ways.

Some fence and railing castings were basically imitations of ornate stone balusters. Others were tracery. Regardless of the design theme, cast iron fences and railings tended to be somewhat massive, using repetitive design elements. The elements were not as thin and muscular as wrought iron elements. But during the latter half of the 19th century, wrought iron was used far less than cast iron for fences or exterior railings. Cast iron was much cheaper. (2-5, 2-6, 2-7) Cast iron fencing and some railings came in regular lengths. They were just bolted or screwed together. But even with cast iron fencing, gates were frequently of wrought iron.

Drawn wire was also used. The wires ranged from 1/8″ to 1/2″ in diameter. They were bent, shaped and interwoven. Wire fence manufacturers Hutchinson & Wickersham, of New York, developed a patented method for "casting the solid rosettes upon the rod at the point of intersection without the aid of rivets." They also cast the surmounting pickets directly on the railings.[6] (4-5) Philadelphia's Wickersham & Walker patented another method of manufacturing wire fencing.

Tastes changed near the end of the century. Cast iron and drawn wire fences and railings tended to fall from favor. People preferred simpler designs of wrought iron, sometimes combined with cast iron features and gate posts. (4-13) Unfortunately, many fine decorative fences were lost to the scrap metal drives during the two world wars.

Although fences and railings had much in common in their design and were frequently made from identical patterns, they had different functions. Railings did not define properties or contain animals. They were safety devices. They kept people from falling off of bridges, porches, balconies, fire escapes, or out of French windows. Stair railings helped unstable persons mount the steps. Moreover, when the front steps were covered with snow and ice, iron railings helped prevent slipping. As a further safety measure, some front step railings even had shoe scrapers cleverly inserted into their ironwork. (4-14)

While their designs were frequently similar, fencing and stair railings exhibited one big difference. Fences were designed for use on horizontal planes. Stair or step railings were intended to be used on slopes. Such railings never looked right when they seemed to be sliding down the slopes of the adjacent stairways or steps. See Chapter 10, *Good Ironwork Practice*.

After 1850, the Philadelphia elite settled in the Rittenhouse Square area. These people indicated their good taste and wealth with exquisite railings on the marble or brownstone front steps leading to their homes. Although most of the adjoining small front gardens and their surrounding fences are gone, the doorways, the stone steps, and the railings leading to those houses survive. The Rittenhouse Square area is a treasure trove of fine front step iron railings. Some of these combined brass with the iron – an elegant aggregation.

Ebenezer Maxwell Mansion, 4-1
200 W. Tulpehocken Street
Attributed to Joseph C. Hoxie (1814-1870), Architect

Ebenezer Maxwell, a Philadelphia merchant, built this house in 1859. Today it is a carefully restored Victorian house museum and resource center, set in a period garden. The style of the house is transitional, from Gothic Revival to Second Empire, embodying features from both idioms. Typical of both periods, the appearance of a highly visible roof is important. Here the architect designed a mansard and ornamented it with a pattern formed by slates of diverse colors. A cast iron fence, facing the sky, surmounts the mansard of the tower. The fence is called a "roof cresting." Its aesthetic purpose was to soften the line between the building and the sky. Since cast iron crestings were popular features on both Gothic Revival and Second Empire style buildings, a cresting was almost inevitable for this fashionable house.[7] (The lightning rod is a later addition.)

Capt. John Meany House, 4-2
(The Joseph Bonaparte House)
260 South 9th Street
Architect unknown

A Franklin Fire Insurance Company survey indicates that this c.1813 building was originally a "two story house with a garrett." An 1891 survey indicates that it had been enlarged and was now a Second Empire house, with a "full 3 floors including a mansard." From 1816 to 1818, it was the home of Joseph Bonaparte, the brother of Napoleon I. Joseph had been King of Naples and later King of Spain. The house has a garden to the south, graced by this handsome fence. Here used on a garden wall, such fences, with Gothic tracery and quatrefoil crosses, were particularly popular around family burial plots, churchyards, and parsonages. The garden gate is complicated and interesting. The leaves just under the top rail are not on the plane of the balance of the unit. Probably stampings, they extend outward. Since the basic design of gate is simply repetitive, it could be adapted to almost any opening width.

Family Burial Plot Fence, 4-3
Laurel Hill Cemetery
3922 Ridge Avenue

Yellow fever plagued Philadelphia a number of times. We now know that the disease is transmitted by the bite of a female Aedes aegypt mosquito. However, in the 1830s, one of the many erroneous theories which developed, was that the plague was connected to noxious fumes, rising from the decaying bodies buried within the city's church yards.[8] A movement sprang up to promote burials outside the city. Advocates suggested "removing the dead from the midst of the dense population of our cities, and placing them in operation with the beautiful works of nature."[9] Consequently, two magnificent suburban estates, flanking the Schuylkill River, were converted into cemeteries. They were Laurel Hill, which was adapted in 1836, and The Woodlands, which became a cemetery in 1843. Although Philadelphia has engulfed them since then, both cemeteries were outside the city when they were established. Since burials were no longer being made adjacent to the churches, some churches bought portions of the suburban cemeteries and sold individual plots to parishioners. With burials now away from the churches, many families felt it especially important to signify their continuing allegiance to their faiths. To accomplish this, they frequently surrounded their family burial plots with "religious" fences, such as were often used around rectories and churchyards. This fence and the fence shown in figure 4-2 are typical of such fences. They incorporate religious symbols – the quatrefoil, said to represent the Cross, and the Gothic arch. Inasmuch as subject "religious" fence was here being used in a cemetery, small castings of funerary urns were added. Laurel Hill Cemetery has the distinction of being the first cemetery in the country to become a National Historic Landmark. Regarding the numerous iron fences which formerly defined family burial plots in older cemeteries, few of them remain. Many fine decorative fences were lost when patriotic citizens donated them to scrap metal drives during the two world wars. The donated fences were remelted and reincarnated into armaments. The cemetery companies were not necessarily unhappy about these removals. Without fences, it was easier to cut the grass!

Drexel Mansion, 4-4
(Now Sigma Chi Fraternity House)
3809 Locust Walk
Thomas Roney Williamson (1852-1896), Architect

This typical Queen Anne style mansion was built in 1884 for the wealthy, socially prominent Drexel family. The repetitive, richly decorative panels forming its wrought iron fence, are well in keeping with the mansion's abundantly embellished architecture. The twisted strong verticals between the panels provide harmonious punctuation points. Unfortunately, the fence manufacturer made a mistake. For the top rail, he bedded two pieces of ironwork on each other. While this defect is not shown in the photograph, some pieces have rusted and pulled apart. (See discussion of this in the Chapter 10: "Good Ironwork Practice.")

154 West Tulpehocken Street, 4-5
Architect unknown

A "Gothic Cottage," built c.1858, "this pretty house shows the artistic suggestion of Downing and other cottage designers, but with the breadth and dignity of Quaker Philadelphia."[10] *The architect applied this drawn wire fence and gate. The fence manufacturer, probably Wickersham, bent the wires to form a pattern. Then he applied solid rosette castings at the points of intersection and cast the surmounting pickets directly upon the railings. The pattern of the gate is slightly reminiscent of a Gothic rose window.*

Fairmount Waterworks Balustrade, 4-6
Schuylkill River near 25th and Spring Garden Streets
Frederick C. Graff (1774-1847), Architect-Engineer
Alterations by Frederick C. Graff, Jr. (1817-1890)

The Classic temple-like peristyle shelter atop this structure conceals the fact that below it is one of the engineering marvels of its time – the Fairmount Waterworks. It supplied the city with water from 1815 to 1909. The entire assembly is both a National Historic Landmark and a National Mechanical Engineering Landmark. Thanks to the Waterworks, when Charles Dickens visited America in 1842, he marveled at the fact that one could go to the top floor of Philadelphia's tallest building, turn on a spigot and get water![11] In the 1860s the level of the terrace was raised and the peristyle shelter was built. Here the architect-engineer was Frederick C. Graff, Jr., son of the Waterworks original designer. As an accessory to the peristyle, a standard Classic Revival balustrade was used. It blends well with the structure. Even though the balustrades are Classical, since the Waterworks was state-of-the-art engineering, it is not surprising that Graff, Jr. had the balustrade produced by state-of-the-art iron casting. More recently, the railing was in bad need of repair. Working with architect John Milner, Robinson Iron restored the railing in 1988. Such balustrades were usually painted stone colors with a sanded paint. Consequently, they appeared to be stone.

Fairmount Park Railing Near Spring Garden Street Bridge, 4-7

This railing was installed along the path leading to the lower level of the long-gone 1874 double decked iron bridge over the Schuylkill River. A similar railing was installed on top of the nearby bluff overlooking the Waterworks. Both of these railings appear to have been made of many component parts which were riveted together.

St. Andrew's Protestant Episcopal Church, 4-8
(*Now the Greek Orthodox Cathedral of St. George*)
250-256 South 8th Street
John Haviland, Architect

This was John Haviland's own church. He designed this handsome Greek Revival structure in 1823. Haviland based his design on the Greek Temple of Bacchus at Teos.[12] Undoubtedly he worked from Stuart and Revett's monograph of meticulous measured drawings, "The Antiquities of Athens." Haviland also designed the impressive cast iron fence.[13] It illustrates how many 19th century architects chose or designed fences to reflect the character of the buildings they were to surround. Haviland used purely Greek motifs such as the anthemion or honeysuckle pattern to cap alternating vertical rods. For the box fence posts he used Greek key designs, surmounting them with Medusa's heads. The entire assembly shows how decorative cast iron can be. In 1921, the Greek Orthodox congregation bought the church and changed its name. The Grecian design theme of the building and fence is appropriate indeed for the present Greek-American congregation.

146 West Tulpehocken Street, 4-9
Architect unknown

After the railroads made it convenient to commute from Germantown to downtown Philadelphia, Germantown became a fashionable suburb. West Walnut Lane and Tulpehocken Street illustrate this. Spacious houses with handsome gardens developed in the areas near the railroad stations. This 2 1/2 story "Gothic Cottage" was built c.1858. Like many of its neighbors, it has an iron fence. Its handsome cast iron fence has overlapping ovals and quatrefoil borders, all with sculptural details. The fence terminates at a pair of majestic fence posts. The maker realized that a gate of the same heavy pattern would be difficult to swing. Consequentially, he produced a decorative iron gate of far lighter members.

Stone-Meredith-Penrose House, 4-10
700 South Washington Square
Architect unknown

This genteel house was built in 1818 for merchant Asaph Stone. The exquisite, graceful wrought iron railings framing the front entrance steps and stoop form a perfect introduction to this elegant dwelling. On them, one can see true wrought iron welding. It produces a different type of joint from today's oxy-acetylene or electric welding. (See 5-18)

Stone-Meredith-Penrose House, 4-11
700 South Washington Square
Architect unknown

The solid and forceful 7th Street castings are in sharp contrast to the wrought iron front step railings. Here, each cast panel is essentially a vigorous, handsome composition of "C"scrolls, set within a simple, explicit frame. The supporting newels are strong, structurally. Their profile is reminiscent, in miniature, of the profile of the Eiffel Tower. In 1967-1968, the author restored and adapted this house to serve as the residence of the British Consul General. It is now privately owned.

William Marks House, 4-12
2227 Green Street
Architect unknown

This c.1885 Victorian brownstone was built for William Marks, a merchant. It is eclectic, even to its appealing and unusual cast iron garden fence. That fence uses asymmetrical "C" scrolls in two directions bent to resemble budding foliage. The "C" scrolls are in juxtaposition to fully opened, erect floral units. Here again, "C" scrolls are more than decoration. They actually brace the fence.

6119 McCallum Street, 4-13
Architect unknown

Late in the 19th century, tastes moved away from elaborate castings. The hairpin fence became popular. At times, some small decorative castings were introduced into the design. Here the gate posts and rosettes are castings.

Allen H. Reed Houses, 4-14
1721-23 Pine Street
Brown & Day (1887-1892), Architects

Both these houses were built in 1888. Eclectic in design, they combine Gothic Revival and Queen Anne features and show a strong influence by the Arts and Crafts Movement. The design of the railings is a charming, delicate wrought iron composition. It combines square rods, twisted rods, a variety of scrolls, and even includes a shoe scraper. It fits in admirably with the architectural style of the houses.

Randolph Wood House, 4-15
321 South 20th Street
Architect unknown

Dated at c.1890, this 3 1/2-story house is Queen Anne in style. Its entrance stoop railing is ornamented by a particularly rich rendition, in wrought iron, of an almost lace-like decoration. Cleverly, the unit utilizes circular motifs as central design elements on both the horizontal and sloping portions. They are surrounded by scrolls of different sizes, which are joined to each other creatively. The strong newels serve as punctuation points.

Isaac Lea Residence, 4-16
(Now Offices of Berger & Montague, P.C.)
1622 Locust Street
John Notman, Architect

In 1852, Notman designed this mansion for Lea, an important scientist and naturalist. That was just after he, Notman, completed the noteworthy Gothic St. Mark's Church, directly across the street. Here, on this stately Italianate dwelling, he applied the pictured refined, Italian Renaissance-inspired cast iron railing. Mounting it on the plain ashlar brownstone wall, it is like an exquisite delicate, piece of jewelry on a simple, elegant dress.

John Eisenbrey, Jr. House, 4-17
1818 Spruce Street
John C. Farr, Builder

This Italianate house was built in 1855. The original railings at the first floor windows and the basement window grilles below, are in sharp contrast to the contemporary flimsy, characterless grilles added to the windows. The basement window grilles are particularly notable for the effortless way in which they fit into the arched tops of the masonry openings. Contrast these grilles with the basement window grilles, capped with truncated circles, shown on 6-9, or the grilles with the weak scrolls atop them in 10-3.

2112 Locust Street, 4-18
Architect unknown

Erected c. 1870, this vernacular dwelling was provided with a Colonial Revival frontispiece some years later. However, the quite sophisticated cast iron stair railing appears to date to the 1870s. An unusual feature is the skillful way its cartouche-like focal feature is modified on the rake. Also, the Greek key borders are adapted cleverly to follow the rake of the steps – a refined, expert touch. Instead of running the same detail down the sloping portion of the railing, the designer skillfully adjusted the Greek key to the descent. As he marched the keys down the slopes, he kept the verticals truly vertical, but sloped the normally horizontal portions of the keys to follow the rake of the steps.

Randolph Wood House, 4-19
1920 Spruce Street
(Now the Academy of Vocal Arts)
Attributed to Furness & Hewitt (1877-n.d.), Architects

Erected c. 1870, this Second Empire building was a natural choice for its current use. In 1902, it had a two-story music room added in the rear.[14] That room lends itself beautifully to the Academy, for its performances. The wrought iron railing in front may have been in place when the building was still a fashionable private residence. Happily, the decorative and stylized lyre form of railing is appropriate for the Academy.

2014 Delancey Place, 4-20
Newman and Harris (1903-1911), Alteration Architects

The quiet distinction of this 3 1/2 story double house is characteristic of this refined block. The railing echoes the dignity of the house. Its Georgian design ancestry is quite evident. For its top border, the judicious, restrained use of the Vitruvian scroll, or running dog motif, is most tasteful. Spherical brass finials formerly existed atop the newels, contributing to the rail's beauty and grace, but sadly, they have disappeared.

Charles Stuart Wood Packard House, 4-21
324 South 21st Street (Northwest Corner at Delancey Place)
Newman and Harris, Architects
Louis Magaziner, A.I.A. (1878-1956), Designer

Built for the financier who headed the bank formerly in the Packard Building, this Neo-Georgian house was erected in c.1906. Its restrained Georgian railing includes decorative panels at selected locations. The small "S" scrolls on each tread add a delightful note. The box newels, with their brass finials, add a touch of elegance. The double stairway and platform would look heavy, were it not for the insertion of the graceful arch below the platform. Aside from its aesthetic appeal, the archway opening also admits light into the basement. Appropriately, its grille is treated with great simplicity.(Yellin's gates for the bank are pictured as 1-10)

Anthony J. Drexel Housing, 4-22
409 South 40th Street
Attributed to George W. & William D. Hewitt, Architects

Drexel, a business leader, developed these houses in 1884. The porches were added at the turn of the century. This railing illustrates how the insertion of an interesting central feature can convert an ordinary piece of wrought ironwork into one that is quite handsome.

Henry House, 4-23
2100 Locust Street
Robert Gray Kennedy (1850-1913), Architect

A fine Queen Anne mansion, this one was built in 1889. The railing provides a note of sophistication at the entrance. It is both unique and highly decorative. The large central oval element, the cartouche, is a favorite feature in later French Renaissance ornament. Note how well the width of the central panel of the railing cooridinates with the width of the basement window below.

91

Emlen Hutchinson House, 4-24
2006 Delancey Place
Cope & Stewardson (1886-1912), Alteration Architects

This is one of the group of houses erected in c.1865 by John McCrea, builder. The pictured decorative front step railing was probably designed by Cope & Stewardson as part of the alterations for Hutchinson. It is quite appropriate for the Georgianesque Victorian residence which it serves. Its reference to classical form is most fitting for the architecture. The railing bears a striking resemblance to the c.1775 stair railing at No. 1 Bedford Square, London, designed by Thomas Leverton.[15]

Francis W. Kennedy House, 4-25
1922 Spruce Street
Frank Miles Day (1861-1918), Architect

Day, a most capable architect, designed this house in 1889. He was obviously influenced by that great architect, Henry Hobson Richardson (1838-1886), who popularized the architectural style now called Richardson Romanesque. Characteristically, Day used heavily rusticated stone, a wide arch, deep recesses, and florid Romanesque type ornament. Here, in both the masonry and wrought ironwork, he contrasted plain areas with richly ornamented ones. Both the handsome cellar window grille and the stair railing exhibit this concept. The railing is punctuated with decorative, robust fence posts or newels.

Dr. Joseph Beale's House, 4-26
1805 Delancey Place
Architect unknown

The houses on the 1800 and 2000 blocks of Delancey Place are among the most elegant dwellings in Philadelphia. While the houses at 1805 and 1807 are very different today, they were built as a pair of Italianate residences in 1857. This floral railing is an interesting example of how a casting pattern for a level area could be adjusted skillfully to adapt it to a slope. By handling the right and left halves of the repeat pattern separately, the foundry man was able to adjust the pattern readily. Thus, he was able to have the railing units go down the slope effortlessly and gracefully. They stand erect as they descend. It is unfortunate that the railing stops short of the stair's run. Contrast this railing with the one in 10-5.

Dr. John A. Elkinton House, 4-27
1018 Clinton Street
Architect unknown

This house was erected in 1840. Its delicate and beautiful railing uses the Vitruvian scroll or running dog motif as a tasteful border for what is essentially a field of cross bars, resembling the letter X. The little "C" scrolls perform admirably as transitional elements in the design between the curvaceous borders and the plain lines of the "Xes."

Ada E. M. Thomas House, 4-28
301 South 21st Street (2044 Spruce Street)
George Watson Hewitt and William D. Hewitt, Architects

Built in 1889 and designed by Frank Furness's former partner, this Second Empire style mansion was later the home of the Philadelphia County Medical Society. Next, it housed the New School of Music. Today it is again a private residence. The building's cast iron railing is Neo-Grec, including a highly stylized floral decoration. It has some of the vigor and eclecticism so characteristic of Furness and Hewitt architecture.

Edmund Lewis House, 4-29
30 South 22nd Street
Hazelhurst & Huckel (1884-1899), Architects

Another Queen Anne style residence, this one was built c.1888.[16] Besides being aesthetically pleasing, the design of the wrought iron front railing of the house is clever. The elongated "S" scroll motif lends itself equally well to use on both the horizontal plane of the landing and the rake of the steps.

Part of the Hockley Development Row, 4-30
239-241 South 21st Street
Furness, Evans & Co. (1886-1928), Architects

These houses are part of a row of four houses built for Thomas Hockley. The National Register of Historic Places says that these 1885 houses: "mark a transition from the 1870's Ruskinian Gothic mode toward a highly personal and expressive style based on the expression of constructive process and the nature of the materials used. Against this austere and demanding form, the overlay of Furness's exuberant ornament, ironwork and woodwork humanize and enliven the buildings. It remains one of the most important of Furness' surviving work." These opposite hand twin houses form the center of the row. Not only are the houses different from those, that flank them, but so is their ironwork. Topped by strong hand rails, the stair railings use twisted and wavy square rods and incorporate strong newels.

Part of the Hockley Development Row, 4-31
237 South 21st Street
Furness, Evans & Co. Architects

Not only is this house different from the other three houses in the Hockley Development, but so is its ironwork. As is typical of all of Furness's creations, the entrance stoop wrought iron railings are certainly distinctive.

Philadelphia Bourse, 4-32
10-20 South 4th Street
George W. & William D. Hewitt, Architects

The Bourse was modeled after similar institutions in Hamburg, Germany; and Manchester, England. Its architects were selected by an "open anonymous competition limited to the architects having offices in the city."[17] In 1979-1981, architects H2L2 (1976—) converted the building to shops and offices. They removed the original atrium skylight that had been just above the mezzanine and added a new one at the roofline. They added an intermediate mezzanine and relocated the two highly decorative original interior wrought iron stairs into the atrium.The stairs get their embellishment from the iron railings. Their designer used the circular motif cleverly as the central feature of each of the repetitive units. By changing the scroll arrangement around it, he adapted it to the rake of the stairs and also to the horizontal landings. The brass handrails add a touch of elegance. The entrance gate to the Bourse is 5-4.

Stairs to the Grand Ballroom, 4-33
The Bellevue-Stratford Hotel, (Now the Park Hyatt Hotel)
200 South Broad Street
George W. & William D. Hewitt, Architects

Opened in 1904, this French Renaissance style building was one of the world's most prestigious hostelries, and opulence was evident everywhere. In 1910, a Philadelphia banker invited a Pittsburgh friend to come to Philadelphia for a visit: "I want you to come to Philadelphia to see the Bellevue. To come to Philadelphia and not see it, is like going to Egypt and missing the pyramids." The Bellevue hosted royalty and every American president, from Theodore Roosevelt to Gerald Ford. For years the famed ballroom on the second floor has been the center of the city's social life. The grand stairway leading to it introduces people to the grandeur and elegance they are about to encounter above. While Center City hosts a number of stairways with fine cast iron railings, this is one of the few such stairways accessible to the public.[18]

GATES AND DOORS

Chapter 5

The gates are mine to open, as the gates are mine to close.

Kipling, Our Lady of the Snows

Gates are generally defensive devices; however many property owners had them turned into handsome objects of art. In early America, iron gates were hand wrought. Later, during the cast iron period, many gates were cast. Then in the 1900s, wrought iron gates reappeared. This section includes not only gates but also grilled iron doors. Such doors are essentially gates, with a sheet of glass behind the iron grilles.

Otto Eisenlohr Mansion, 5-1
(Now the official residence of the President of the University of Pennsylvania)
3812 Walnut Street
Horace Trumbauer (1868-1938), Architect

Reminiscent of High Renaissance country seats in France, this 1911 mansion was built for Eisenlohr, a wealthy cigar manufacturer. The richly embellished, elaborate gateway is in keeping with the architecture of the building. Eisenlohr's initial letter "E" is used in the gates. It is also inserted into the iron cartouche above them where it is used in a normal way and is reversed as well. The wrought iron gateway successfully combines straight members with a variety of "C" and "S" scrolls and other curving pieces. The adjoining spear fence is quite defensive.

Rodin Museum, 5-2, facing page
NE Corner, 22nd Street and Benjamin Franklin Parkway.
Paul Philippe Cret, F.A.I.A. (1876-1945), Architect
Jacques Auguste Henri Greber, (1882-1962) Landscape
Architect

In 1905, the great French sculptor Auguste Rodin (1840-1917) purchased the ruins of the Chateau d'Issy. He intended to restore it as a
museum to house his growing collection of ancient art. However,
because of the great expense involved, he decided to preserve only the
entrance. In 1907, he had it reconstructed at his home in Meudon.
Today it overlooks his grave, which is graced with his famous sculptural
work, "The Thinker." [1] Philadelphian Jules Mastbaum, president of a
chain of moving picture theaters, acquired a large collection of Rodin's
sculptures and drawings. Once, when in Paris, Mastbaum met landscape architect Greber and commissioned him to prepare sketches for a
small museum to house his, Mastbaum's, Rodin collection. He told
Greber that he wanted a garden at the entrance and suggested that the
garden gate be a replica of the Chateau d'Issy architectural fragments,
that Rodin had assembled at his Meudon studio.[2] Greber enlisted his
friend, Paul Cret, as his collaborator. Working from Greber's sketches,
Cret's office prepared the actual construction drawings.[3] Complete
with its ironwork, they used the Chateau façade replica as the entrance
to the garden in front of the museum building. The replica flanks the
Parkway. The frame of the gateway and the gates themselves appear to
be mostly wrought iron. However, the gates do embody some cast
ornaments. The author of the original ironwork is not known. While it
is simplified, it has a resemblance to the ironwork by Hugh Brisville,
who was a locksmith in Paris, about 1663.[4] The Rodin Museum was
erected with Mastbaum's funds and completed in 1929. Both the building and its collection were turned over to the City and are administered
by the Art Museum.

329 South 21st Street, 5-3
Architect unknown

It is probable that this gateway is contemporary wrought iron. It is certainly far more handsome than most gateways being produced today. Of
especial interest is the arched unit above the gate. A circular cartouche
grows out of the curvilinear design and provides a place for a lantern.

Gates at the Philadelphia Bourse, 5-4
10-20 South 4th Street
George W. & William D. Hewitt, Architects

These richly embellished wrought iron gates stand outside the eastern end of the Bourse. In both scale and design, they blend beautifully with the building's 1893 architecture. (The interior stairway is figure 4-32.)

Lea and Febiger Building, 5-5
600 South Washington Square, (Now the Marian Locks Gallery)
Earle Nelson Edwards (1888-1969), Architect
Samuel Yellin, Artist-blacksmith

Lea and Febiger was the nation's oldest publishing firm. It was founded in 1785. In 1923, it built this Second Renaissance Revival structure.[5] While these entrance gates were created for the original owners, they are even more appropriate for the present occupant, an art gallery. Yellin's gates are themselves works of art. They are so delicate, that one hardly realizes that they are actually protective.

First Unitarian Church, 5-6 facing page, 5-7
2125 Chestnut Street, at Van Pelt Street
Furness, Evans & Co., Architects

Furness designed this eclectic church, which was built between 1883 and 1886. Its exterior has been greatly altered. The steeple structure, which included a covered entryway, was removed. Also, an early photograph at the Historical Commission seems to show doors where these gates are today. Whether the building gates were designed by Furness or by a later architect, is of secondary importance. In any case they are so handsome that one almost forgets that they are there to protect the building they embellish. The above mentioned early photograph does show the current garden gates, which were undoubtedly designed by Furness. They are both defensive and distinctive. While they are as protective as conventional spear fence gates would be, they appear to be more friendly. The leaf-like tops of the vertical members seem particularly appropriate for garden gates. Furness always developed unusual and highly personal solutions to architectural problems.

Richard Cadwalader House, 5-8
2019 Delancey Place
Dearmond, Ashmead & Bickley (1911-1929), Architects

This 1860 dwelling was refaced and heightened in 1918. With its present elegant façade, the house eventually became the home of the late author, humanitarian, activist, Nobel Prize winner, Pearl S. Buck. Its façade, a Beaux-Arts design, gets its distinction from having large plain areas of ashlar stonework contrasting with judiciously placed restrained, sophisticated decoration. Its wrought iron grille is primarily a series of scrolls, combined cleverly. An interesting feature is the way the mail slot was worked into the door's fabric. Of course, the grille is defensive. However, it is treated so ingeniously that it appears to be only a friendly artistic element.

George Fox House, 5-9
343 South 18th Street
Architect unknown

While it was already a stylish residence in its previous incarnation, this house received the current Jacobean façade in 1895.[6] Noteworthy is the unusually rich entrance gate. The designer combined the Greek anthemion, the scroll, the circle, the heart, and various other motifs – both conventionally and inverted. Together, they produce a unique and handsome piece of ironwork.

111

L. W. Geise House, 5-10
2100 Delancey Place
Duhring, Okie & Ziegler (1899-1918), Architects

Now an apartment house, this former mansion was erected in 1905. With their restrained but delicate ornament, the attractive door and basement window grilles fit in admirably with the building's Beaux-Arts design. The design of the ironwork may have been influenced by a grille shown in an engraving of the oeuvre of the 17th century Parisian ironworker, Hugh Brisville. [7]

1900 Spruce Street, 5-11
Architect unknown

This imposing Italianate house was built c.1855. Its stately doors gain added richness from the contrasting blank areas in their centers. The handsome transom grille, with the address worked into it, blends beautifully with the door grilles.

113

Edward C. Knight, Jr. House, 5-12
1629 Locust Street
Horace Trumbauer, Architect

While this building serves as offices today, it was erected in 1902-1903 as a fashionable town house. It was one of the most pretentious residences in the Rittenhouse Square area and is the epitome of French Beaux-Arts design.[8] Trumbauer used iron freely, both inside and outside of the mansion. The entrance step railings are a good solution to the safety problem. Their elegant simplicity leads ones eyes to the highly decorative door. The elaborate grille on the iron and glass door is but one example of the eclectic French architectural tradition used throughout. The more dense pattern around the lock is a suitable safety measure. Contrast these railings with those in the photograph 10-10.

Pennsylvania Academy of the Fine Arts, 5-13
118 North Broad Street
Furness and Hewitt (1870-1875), Architects

The Academy, America's oldest art institution, is housed in this National Historic Landmark. Its present structure was erected between 1872 and 1876. The building shows Furness's practice of eclecticism – drawing from many architectural vocabularies and combining them. Here he fused Ruskinian Gothic, with French mansards, Greek type friezes and other influences. Now considered an architectural masterpiece, it is revealing to quote from a comment on the building, which appeared in 1876.... "By far the most interesting element in the recent building of Philadelphia is Mr. Furness's work. Nobody would think of calling it commonplace, and it is so far from being scholastic that a good deal of it is hard to classify.... It is the work of an architect full of spirit and invention, who has not yet reached the prime of his powers."[9] Furness used cast iron freely. On the exterior, he embodied a cast iron truss into the Cherry Street façade. On the interior, he used exposed decorative cast iron columns to support cast iron beams, which are spanned by segmental brick vaults. This was the last word in 1870s fire-resistive construction. Like the rest of the building, the gates are "hard to classify" in style. They are early examples of Furness's highly personal representations of floral forms. Often hidden, the gates slide into pockets when the galleries are open.

Venez Voir, 5-14
(Now the Office of J. David Hoffman, M.D.)
2050 Locust Street
Architect unknown

*In the 1920s, Venez Voir converted this 1897 dwelling to commercial use. More recently, a physician converted it
again, this time making it into his offices. The pictured charming, delicate entrance door grille with its bird motif is
one of the few Art Deco grilles in the city not on a high rise building.*

Pedestrian Entrance Gate, 5-15
Woodlands Cemetery
Woodland Avenue at 40th Street
Paul Philippe Cret, F.A.I.A., Architect

It was Paul Cret who first made the
University of Pennsylvania's school of architecture an institution of national standing and
who received the American Institute of
Architects' Gold Medal. He emigrated from
France in 1903 and lived a stone's throw
from this cemetery, where he is now buried.
Cret was the architect for a number of the
World War I monuments in the European
battlefield cemeteries. The architect of many
important monumental buildings, his favorite
design source was Classical Greek architecture. However, he adapted it, creatively, into
a personal style.[10] For this door, he used the
cast iron Greek anthemion as the grille's
design motif, standing it in the normal way
and then up-ending it.

Farmers' and Mechanics' Bank, 5-16
*(Now American Philosophical Society's
Benjamin Franklin Hall)*
427 Chestnut Street
John Myers Gries (1827-1862), Architect

*This structure was erected in 1854-55, shortly before
the Civil War, the war in which the building's gifted,
rising young architect lost his life.[11] Gries' richly
ornamented doors were even more protective than
mere iron grilles. Embellished with fierce lions to
guard the treasures within, the doors themselves are
iron, part plate and part cast. Because of the security
they afforded, iron doors were most appropriate for
this structure, originally an Italianate style bank. The
doors protected large sums of money. Even though
the doors are no longer operative, and the building is
no longer a bank, it continues to house treasures.
Many of the historic documents housed within are far
more valuable than money – they are priceless. The
eastern door of the pair, the one in the photograph,
has a small applied casting at its base, reading Ridge
Avenue. Small holes at the base of the other door
indicate that there was an applied casting at the base
of that door as well. Since the Robert Wood Foundry
excelled in such complicated castings and since that
foundry was on Ridge Avenue, an educated guess
would be that the missing applied casting read Robert
Wood Foundry.*

2133 Walnut Street, 5-17
Architect unknown

This once luxurious townhouse was built c.1870 and was like its neighbors. Its façade was completely reworked c.1910. The entrance doorway could easily be supplanted in Paris. The magnificent door and transom grille blend beautifully with the stone carvings surrounding them. The grilles are iron, as are the doors and transom frames.

Reformed Protestant Episcopal Church, 5-18
(Now the Evangelical Lutheran Church of the Holy Communion)
Chestnut and Van Pelt Streets
Isaac Pursell (1853-1910), Architect

The Lutheran sect goes back to 16th century Germany and so does the German Renaissance use of thin round iron rods to form gates and grilles. Such rods were easily shaped, bent and welded. While the flanking grilles shown here incorporate bars, the gates are formed from thin round iron rods. Thus, the designer of these attractive gates returned to German Renaissance roots for the inspiration of his ironwork. Although this church is an 1889 structure, its grilles and entrance gates are contemporary and are products of modern welding. Contrast these welds with the true wrought iron welds shown in 4-10.

Cast Iron Gate to a Cemetery Lot, 5-19

This photo of a gate for a cemetery fence is from the c.1845 Robert Wood catalog. It is a good illustration of the type of iron-work in which foundries excel. The gate is replete with symbols of mourning for lost family members. The lambs and doves are melancholy and even the willow tree is weeping.

WINDOW AND DOOR GRILLES

Chapter 6

If there are grilles they should be serving as screens, not merely bolted to a blank wall. If within the grille there are ornaments, quatrefoils, scrolls, etc., they should be integral parts of the grille itself, so that at a glance it is evident that they are not merely stuck on for the sake of being pretty.

Gerald K. Geerlings, *Wrought Iron in Architecture.*

Defensive iron grilles are nothing new. They appear on buildings as dispersed as the great Florentine palazzi of the Renaissance, the Hotel Carnavalet in Paris, and Castle Cary in Scotland. Throughout the ages, countless architects employed them on innumerable buildings. But competent architects and ironworkers have always made them more than merely protective devices; they have made them into decorative features of the buildings.

During the period covered by this book, many buildings were equipped with defensive ironwork grilles. Some were wrought – the ironsmiths employing round, square, or rectangular members. They twisted them, bent them, and wove them. Other grilles were cast, frequently with highly decorative surface ornament. In the book on metals in America's historic buildings, the late Harley J. McKee, F.A.I.A., wrote: "Although little noticed, there is a seemingly endless variety of decorative cellar window grilles in Philadelphia. With the first-floor level several feet above grade and the sidewalks often extending right up to the façade, these articulated iron grilles were installed to protect exposed cellar windows while still allowing ventilation." [1]

One of the most popular casting patterns for basement window grilles was the rinceau, which is of Roman origin.[2] It consists of foliage scrolls, usually of the acanthus leaf. Then there were other patterns using the acanthus leaf, patterns which were both decorative and opaque. Because of its large areas of surface embellishment, the acanthus was particularly fitted for being cast. But whether they utilized the acanthus or some other decorative feature and whether they were wrought or cast, many grilles were pleasing in appearance.

With so much crime today, more and more people are incorporating defensive, secure ironwork grilles on their doors and windows. Unfortunately, many people simply settle for a series of bars, making jail cells of their rooms. With a little imagination and a small additional cost, the property owners could obtain grilles, which are both secure and attractive. Furthermore, good-looking grilles increase a building's value, both aesthetically and monetarily.

Following are some examples of ironwork that is just as protective as today's jail-like bars, however, this ironwork is tastefully pleasing as well.

Penn Mutual Building, 6-1
Southeast Corner, 6th and Walnut Streets
Edgar Viguers Seeler (1867-1929), Architect

This 1913 building was the first of the series of three Penn Mutual buildings facing Independence Square. It is a product of the Neo-Classic style which was popular early in the 20th century. The chaste protective iron grilles fit in well with the disciplined Roman Revival architecture surrounding them.

American Baptist Publication Society, 6-2
(Now Juniper East Apartments)
1329-39 Lombard Street
Architect Unknown

This 1895 building alludes to Richardson Romanesque. Greatly altered, it retains a number of its original window grilles. While the grilles vary with the sizes of the openings, all are attractive. They combine ingenious wrought iron "C" scrolls, "S" scrolls, and spirals, along with straight rods.

Fidelity Mutual Life Insurance Building, 6-3
(Now Reliance Standard Life Insurance Company Building)
25th Street and Fairmount Avenue
Zantzinger, Borie and Medary, Architects

One of Philadelphia's finest examples of Art Deco architecture, this building was erected in 1925-26. Its architects involved top artists and craftsmen, including Lee Lawrie, the famous sculptor who had embellished the Nebraska State Capitol. The architects designed this handsome wrought iron, that fits in splendidly with the architecture of the building. While it is basically just a series of vertical bars, the judiciously placed ornaments above the top rail convert the grille into a distinctive architectural piece. Until recently, grilles such as these covered all first floor windows. Now they remain only on the end of the building.

126

Philadelphia Saving Fund Society, 6-4
700 Walnut Street
Addison Hutton (1834-1916) of Sloan & Hutton (1866-1868), Architect for the 1868-1869 eastern portion.
Furness, Evans & Company, Architects for the 1897-1898 western portion. [3]

Prior to the 1930-1932 erection of the internationally famous P.S.F.S. building at 12th and Market Streets, this structure was the main office of what had been the oldest savings institution in the nation. The 19th century austere granite building appears to have been designed to symbolize the bank's conservative practices and stability. Following the chaste, rigid architecture, the lower portion of the typical window grille is Spartan and geometric. However, the upper portion is more curvaceous and decorative. That treatment allows the grille to fit effortlessly into the arch, in a way that an upward extension of the vertical rods would not permit.

Philadelphia Museum of Art, 6-5
26th and Benjamin Franklin Parkway
Horace Trumbauer, Charles C. Zantzinger (1872-1954) and Charles L Borie, Jr. (1870-1943), Collaborating Architects

Commonly known as the Art Museum, this commanding structure sits atop the hill called Fairmount, at the northwest end of Benjamin Franklin Parkway. The museum was built between 1919 and 1928 and is one of the nation's finest examples of early-20th-century eclectic Neo-Classicism. There were several collaborating architects. However, the coordinating architect was Borie, and the actual construction drawings were produced in the Trumbauer office. At the start of the project, Julian Abele, (1881-1950) the gifted African-American architect who was Trumbaur's chief designer, is said to have undertaken an extended tour of Greece. He went to study details of its Classical architecture, so as to incorporate them into this monumental building. While he used Classic Greek details as his fountainhead, he interpreted those details freely, to serve contemporary needs. The tops of the window grilles he designed were apparently derived from the distinctive Ionic column capitals in the interior of the Temple of Apollo Epicurius at Bassae, Greece. The Bassae capitals combine the volutes with arched lines above anthemions.[4] For the grilles, Abele simplified the Bassae capitals and interspersed them with spearheads. The result is most successful.

Kensington National Bank, 6-6
(Now a First Union Bank Branch)
2-8 West Girard Avenue
Frank Furness, Architect

Furness built this bank in 1877, shortly after he completed his first masterpiece, the Pennsylvania Academy of the Fine Arts.[5] The Kensington bank is a strongly assertive, barricaded granite building. For its depositors, it symbolized security. As befits such a structure, the ironwork Furness designed for it appears to be impregnable. Here Furness combined protective spears with his favorite stylized floral shapes.

1613 Spruce Street, 6-7
Architect unknown

Erected in 1850, this handsome Italianate house, now offices, is one of a number of fine buildings which enhance Spruce Street. In designing or selecting the pictured ironwork, its architect followed Renaissance design tradition. He provided this delicate and graceful cellar window grille with rich surface decoration. It was a natural for casting.

Davis Residence, 6-8
230 South 21st Street
Architect unknown

This c.1860 vernacular Italianate house has been designated as an Historic Site in Journalism. Richard Harding Davis (1864-1916), famous war correspondent, grew up here. The building had its façade altered about 1910. The designer of the casting used a pleasing floral motif, turned it upside down, and repeated it lengthwise. While the height of the grille was fixed, its width could be adjusted easily.

Samuel Kerr Residence, 6-9
1905 Spruce Street
Architect unknown

This is a Georgian Revival house. Its grille is a perfect example of the use of the rinceau design so popular with the cast iron industry. Casting made it possible and economical to produce the highly decorative surface ornament. This particular cellar grille would look better if the row of small circles at the top decreased in diameter as they moved away from the center. Here there are uniform circles, with their tops amputated.

2022 Spruce Street, 6-10
Architect unknown

This is one of a row of Italianate houses built c.1855. According to the insurance survey for the Fire Association of Philadelphia, it was unoccupied in 1866.[6] Its cast iron basement window grille is both plump and opaque and has much of the character of Roman ornament.[7] While it has none of the muscularity of wrought iron, the rich surface decoration on its acanthus leaves illustrates the type of work which casting does best. The scrolls on top work splendidly to fill in the space above the essentially rectangular design. They have the same type of design weight and surface treatment as the basic design below. Contrast them with the unimaginative filler shown in 10-7 or the filler of truncated circles shown in 6-9.

2135 Spruce Street, 6-11
Architect unknown

This Second Empire style house was built in 1860. Its casting is particularly handsome. The designer used the Greek anthemion assertively and filled in around it sympathetically. The surface decoration is rich and has been crafted to enhance the effect. As is true with all good design, there is a strong statement of the central design theme and everything else is subordinated to it. It certainly works here.

2204 Pine Street, 6-12
Architect unknown

Built c.1860, this is a vernacular Italianate house. The designer of its grille did essentially what architect Paul Philippe Cret did decades later, at Woodlands Cemetery. Both designers used the Greek anthemion twice, turning it in opposite directions. Cret stood the features up vertically. (5-15). The designer of this basement window grille turned the anthemions on their sides. Both results work. The border on the basement window grille harmonizes nicely with the central motif.

Roberts-Quay House, 6-13
1035 Spruce Street
Architect unknown

This pretentious Romano-Tuscan Renaissance Revival mansion was built before 1858, for Edwan Roberts. In 1879, it was purchased by Matthew Quay, an attorney and politician, who became a U. S. Senator. In 1962, its then owner wanted to demolish it. However, it was saved and restored in 1974 and became the Philadelphia Dance Academy. In 1978, it suffered from a fire. Renovated again, it is now a 20-unit apartment house.[8] Its designer "grew" cast iron acanthus plants within a series of freely interpreted classical arches. The small segments of arches, at both the right and left sides of the grille, indicate that the pattern could be extended in both directions to accommodate wider openings. Aesthetically, the grille would have been improved if some small complete features replaced the flanking partial arches.

1911 Spruce Street, 6-14
Architect unknown

According to the date on this French Renaissance structure, this house was built in 1894. Its grille is most graceful and admits a larger than usual amount of light into the basement. While the ironwork serves a different purpose and fills a different sort of space, its inspiration may well have been the iron lamp bracket in Micklegate Hill House, York, England. Its sensuous curves, stylized leaves and decorated borders seem to follow that historical precedent. The historic lamp bracket in York is undoubtedly wrought iron.[9] This wrought iron basement grille has four small floral castings in the corners. However, the resemblance is there.

Hipple House, 6-15
244 South 21st Street
Addison Hutton, Architect

This 1862 house is described in the Pennsylvania Historic Resources Survey as follows: "In the midst of small, simple Italianate houses is [this] tall, richly embellished townhouse. Neo-Grec detail frames the first floor windows, but in good Queen Anne fashion, the second floor explodes with decorative panels."[10] Its admirable wrought iron cellar window grille is reminiscent of a great peacock spreading its tail feathers. As is often the case with really good design, the concept is simple. Here it is just a series of artistically distributed scrolls. Unlike many cellar window grilles, this one allows a maximum amount of light to enter the interior.

C. S. W. Packard House, 6-16
315 South 21st Street
Newman, Woodman & Harris, Architects

The wrought iron basement window grille on this 1903 house illustrates how a simple series of vertical bars can be made interesting by judiciously inserting an ornamental feature. The ornament itself is just a circle, encompassing a series of scrolls. However, its simplicity and clarity fit in admirably with the architecture of the house.

Bishop Mackay-Smith House, 6-17
251 South 22nd Street
Theophilus Parsons Chandler (1845-1928), Architect

Chandler did this house in 1903-4.[11] For the basement, he designed or selected this ornamental but simple wrought iron grille. It is another one that admits maximum light. This grille fits into the space admirably and effortlessly.

Charlton Yarnall House, 6-18
235 South 17th Street
Frank Miles Day & Brother (1893-1909), Architects.
Samuel Yellin, Artist-Blacksmith

Built in 1908, this distinguished former residence now serves as offices. Its basement window grilles with their simple and robust circles and scrolls fit in well with the building's Jacobean Revival architecture. The wrought iron piece was one of Samuel Yellin's first commissions. In his authoritative work "Samuel Yellin, Metalworker," Jack Andrews points out that Yellin took the design from figure 32 in Violet-le-Duc's Dictionnaire Raisonne de l'Architecture Francaise, vol. 6, p. 76.

St. Anthony Club House. 6-19
32 South 22nd Street
Wilson Eyre, Jr., Architect

Eyre, a most gifted architect, designed this clubhouse for the local aristocracy in 1888. A Venetian Revival building, it embodies many of the characteristics of Eyre's sophisticated and individualistic architecture, which culminated in his masterpiece – the University Museum. For this basement window grille, Eyre and his blacksmith took a simple basket weave grille and, by turning it outward, made it into a decorative feature.

142

313 South 22nd Street, 6-20
Architect unknown

The architect who designed this 1885 Queen Anne style house borrowed from various architectural idioms. His handsome front door derives from the Arts and Crafts vocabulary. He combined interesting woodwork with glamorized wrought iron. His extended iron hinges are purely decoration, since a paneled door, such as this, needs no assistance from any ironwork to hold it together. His door grille fits the opening beautifully. Its design could have been inspired by the grille on St. Swithen's Shrine, at Winchester Cathedral in England. [12]

1721 Spruce Street, 6-21
Original
Architect unknown
J. Fuller (fl. 1919-1936) Architect in 1925

This Italianate house, erected in 1850, was modernized by Fuller in 1925. Its handsome and delicate door grille derives from French Renaissance tradition. Perhaps the ironworker who produced it saw a picture of the inlay from the Cardinal's Room in the Castle of Ancy-Le-Franc, in France. Certainly, there is a strong resemblance between that inlay pattern and the pattern of the grille.[13]

Thomas Hockley House, 6-22
235 South 21st Street
Furness and Hewitt, Architects

In 1875, Frank Furness "was just emerging as the leading and most innovative local architect of his generation, [He] applied to this High Victorian Gothic house expressive brick patterns and bold details to make a heavy and uncommon design all the more massive and eccentric.[14] The Hockley House is considered Furness's finest townhouse. According to the Pennsylvania Historical Resources Survey, the house represents "the height of High Victorian originality, combining architectural polychromy with vigorous sculpture." The wrought iron door grilles are characteristic of Furness at this, his most resourceful period. Here he combines a defensive spear design with one of his favorite features, highly stylized floral arrangements. It is obvious that these grilles were designed, specifically for the spaces which they occupy.[15]

MINOR STRUCTURES

Chapter 7

When cast iron verandahs were thought to contribute the ultimate touch of elegance to a residence, builders in the 1840's were apt to make their selections from the comprehensive catalogue of Robert Wood (later Wood & Perot) of Philadelphia. Through the medium of this catalogue – itself a unique venture – the firm's designs "for railings,... and other ornamental architectural iron work" were installed all over the States. Other foundries soon copied their models.

Frances Lichten, Decorative Art of Victoria's Era.

As discussed in this chapter, minor structures are considered to be: porches, balconies, fire escapes, marquees, and canopies.

During the Victorian period a romantic, picturesque movement developed, permeating all the arts, internationally. This is the movement which gave us Chopin and Brahms in music, Durand and Turner in painting, A. J. Downing in landscape design, and Alexander Jackson Davis in architecture.

In cast ironwork, this translated itself into ornamental fences, railings, and treillage. The treillage was used to support marquees, galleries and roofs. Some treillage patterns were architectural in detail, using Classic motifs, or trefoils, and quatrefoils of Gothic origin. However, the most popular treillage patterns were basically floral. Such treillage would simulate rose bushes, honeysuckle, grapevines, or other such plants, climbing their ironhanded way up to the supported structures. Variations in design were easily produced by rearranging the patterns.

Not only theaters but many hotels, apartment houses, and clubs placed marquees at their main entrances. The immediate effect was to make the buildings fashionable. If they were cantilevered or hung, the marquees' supports were usually wrought iron, or later, steel. If they had columnar supports, they were usually cast iron. Generally, they reflected the design idioms of the buildings to which they were appended.

At the domestic scale, cast iron treillage was frequently used to support the roofs of porches or balconies. Among the most notable local examples are the porches on the Tuscan Villa style John Kennedy Mansion, now within Valley Forge National Historical Park. (f-2) Larger houses frequently had conservatories appended to them. Virtually all the conservatories employed cast iron structural members of some type. Also, many larger Victorian gardens featured gazebos or garden pavilions, these frequently utilizing cast iron columns or treillage for their roof support. (9-1)

As mentioned above, another Philadelphia export to New Orleans was an unusual one – cast iron tombs. Tombs were needed because New Orleans' high water table forced all burials to be above ground. Accordingly, Robert Wood and Co. furnished a number of the cast iron mausoleums found in that city's cemeteries.[1]

While Philadelphia's foundries supplied many of the cast iron porches, balconies or galleries throughout the South, especially in New Orleans, few examples remain in the Philadelphia area. They were fairly expensive, so even at the outset they appeared only on homes of the most well-to-do.

William H. Winder Houses, 7-1
234 South 3rd Street
Thomas U. Walter, Architect.

Originally, there were three Winder houses in this group. All were splendid Greek Revival structures. Built between 1843 and 1846, one was demolished years ago. Their magnificent classically inspired balconies, probably the city's finest, had been removed. The balcony on 234, above, had been mounted on a stone wall in Southampton, PA. Architect Charles H. Burnette bought it and installed it on this house, his home. Thomas U. Walter had used these balconies to serve as transitions from the embellished marble of the first floors to restrained brick upper stories. Visually, the balconies divorce the upper floor window openings from the first floor wall openings, because the voids do not line up. The castings on 234 features the griffin, the mythical Greek monster, part lion, part eagle.

William H. Winder Houses, 7-2
232 South 3rd Street
Thomas U. Walter, Architect.

This casting was at the Philadelphia Museum of Art. When Society Hill was being restored, the Art Museum lent its balcony to the Episcopal Community Services, which occupies this building. The design for this balcony, the whippet balcony, comes from plate 8, Roman Ornament for Borders, Pilasters, Friezes in Cottingham's handbook The Smith and Founder's Director. *It was published in London in 1824.*[2]

Michael Bouvier House, 7-3
260 South 3rd Street
Architect unknown

This house is one of a group of brownstone residences built in the Italianate manner in 1848. That was just a few years after architect John Notman introduced the Italianate style when he designed the Athenaeum. The chief embellishments on these austere façades are the highly decorative castings that surround the small balconies. Fittingly, for such pretentious houses, the design of the ironwork is formal.

Schuylkill Hose, Hook & Ladder Company, 7-4
1227 Locust Street
Architect unknown

Like the Hope Engine Company's building (3-7), this c.1857 stately Italianate building was also erected to house a volunteer fire company. It served that group until 1870, when the city took over fire-fighting functions. From 1870 to 1881, it was the home of the Catholic Philopatrian Literary Institute. Later, when it became a restaurant, the façade was violated in innumerable ways, including removal of the balcony. Finally, in 1989, as part of an urban renewal project, the façade was restored to its original appearance.[3] The reborn balcony, with its exquisite railing, indicates that the building is set up like the great Italian palazzi. It has a "piano nobile," i.e., its principal rooms are on the second floor. Similar to the embellished trim on a fine linen tablecloth, the balcony's cast iron railing almost looks like embroidery. It imparts a lighter touch to this aristocratic structure.

151

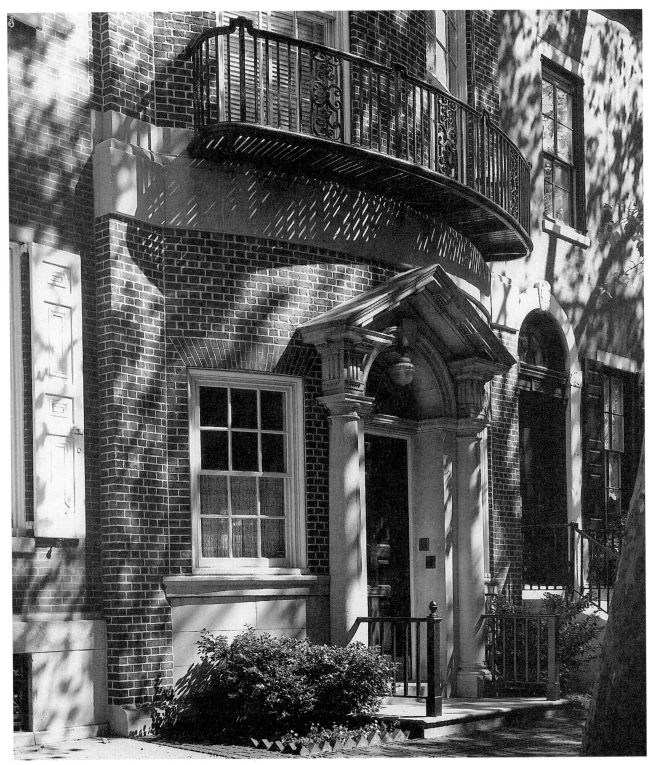

Charles Y. Audenreid House, 7-5
1827 Delancey Place
Charles Barton Keen, Architect

John McCrea originally owned this 1859 house.[4] In 1901, architect Keen provided it with the present Georgian Revival façade. His bowed front wall called for just such a balcony. In keeping with the architecture, the balcony embodies Georgian design motifs. The restrained pattern of the ironwork is appropriate for the balcony's curving shape. The slight rise in the top rail, above the intermediate principal support posts, is a pleasant and sophisticated design feature. The aesthetic effect of the ironwork is enhanced by the interesting shadow it casts.

Thomas Raeburn White House, 7-6
1807 Delancey Place
Edward Edwards (1873-1948), Architect

Built in 1857, the first owner of this house was Samuel Wiltbank. Its façade was originally the opposite hand to 1805 Delancey Place, the twin neighboring house to the east. In 1925, Thomas Raeburn White, who then owned 1807, had the façade of the house reworked following Regency precedent. [5] *Architect Edwards took the circular form of the door head, echoed it in the transoms of the French windows on the second floor, and emphasized it further with the circular balconies. The delicate round shadows which the balconies cast enhance the effect and add a note of richness to the design.* [6] *Had he applied a single rectangular balcony across the front, the entire façade would have been ruined.*

153

Apartment House built for Harry and Elizabeth Platt, 7-7
1200 Spruce Street
Edwin P. Bertollette, Architect (d. 1936)

Although this 1901 apartment house could be called Colonial Revival in style, its un-Colonial fire escapes are an important feature of its design. While most fire escapes are unattractive and mar the appearance of their buildings, these escapes prove that they need not be so. The building is actually decorated by the light, graceful railings and the shadows that the fire escapes cast.

Athenæum of Philadelphia, 7-8
219 South 6th Street
John Notman, Architect

The Athenæum of Philadelphia, a member-supported library and research facility, is one of the great depositories of books and creations of the Victorian age. It is a leading archive of drawings by Philadelphia architects. Having won the Athenæum's architectural competition, John Notman became its architect.[7] His winning façade was undoubtedly influenced by Sir Charles Barry's Italianate style Travellers' Club in London. Built between 1845-47, the Athenæum was one of the country's first two Italianate structures. (The other one, built concurrently, was the long-destroyed A. T. Stewart Downtown Store in New York.)[8] The Italianate exterior notwithstanding, Notman designed the interior in the Greek Revival idiom. The second floor Reading Room is one of the nation's outstanding interiors in that style. Outside that Reading Room is this handsome 1847 cast iron balcony. It overlooks the Victorian garden in the rear and harmonizes well with it. The iron castings here illustrate how various design themes were frequently mixed. The treillage supporting the porch roof is partially Classic and partially floral in design, while the railing is Classic in derivation.

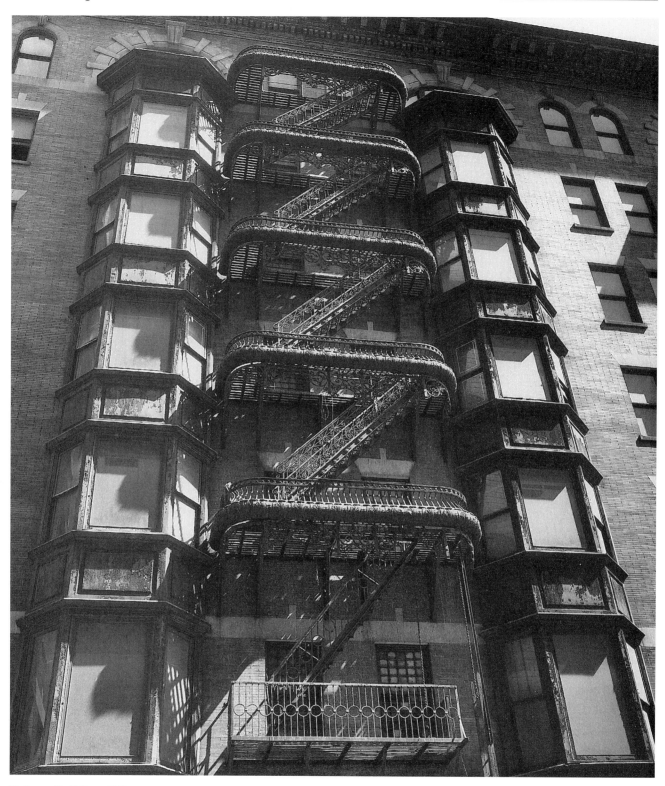

DeLong Building, 7-9
Southeast Corner, 13th and Chestnut Streets
Horace Trumbauer, Architect

The style of this 1899 building is a typical Philadelphia architectural style compromise. While it embodies the then avant garde bay windows typical of the Chicago school of architecture, it retains many traditional Classical features, such as arches, quoins, etc. Here, Trumbauer again proves that fire escapes do not have to be unsightly. Although the escape's railings are fairly simple, they are quite decorative. The supporting brackets add a further bit of ornament.

Spruce Building, Pennsylvania Hospital, 7-10
Northwest Corner of 8th and Spruce Streets
Bartley, Long, Mirenda and Reynolds (1971-1979), Architects

This 1974 building is a replacement for an earlier hospital building on the site. The balconies leading to the fire tower are unique. Instead of design-ing the more usual, uninteresting excrescencies, the architects made the fire balconies and their supporting brackets into highly decorative features. In keeping with building's architecture, the design is of Georgian derivation. Unquestionably later additions, the ugly, unsympathetic, box-like adjacent enclosures are most unfortunate.

The Belgravia, 7-11
1811 Chestnut Street
Milligan & Webber (1897-1910), Architects

Originally an apartment hotel or "pied-a-terre," serving many people listed in the 1904 Social Register,[9] the Belgravia is now an office building. As was befitting a structure serving the elite, it was provided with a marquee in its early days. Because of the haphazard way in which it intersects the flanking columns at the entrance, the marquee appears to have been an afterthought. Its design idiom is French, 18th century. All the iron components are castings.

Wetherill Apartment Building, 7-12
1830 Rittenhouse Square
Frederick Webber, Architect

In 1914, developer Samuel P. Wetherill, Sr. erected this Beaux Arts apartment house on the site of the Thomas Alexander Scott mansion. Now a condominium, it was the first apartment house and first high rise on Rittenhouse Square. Besides providing shelter, the massive glass and cast iron marquee plays an important part in the design of the building. It emphasizes the cornice line above the first floor. That line is the base for the monumental columns and pilasters above. The designer provided a series of decorative wrought iron brackets below the marquee and used a series of antefixes to decorate its top.

3615 Locust Walk, 7-13
Architect unknown

Here is evidence that simple ironwork can also be attractive. These unadorned, modern, rhythmic railings enclose the balconies and are the chief embellishments on the façade of this fraternity house. One advantage of such railings is that they can be lengthened or shortened as needed, and they will still look right.

315 South 18th Street, 7-14, facing page
Architect unknown

This 1850s row house was altered into a Regency Revival dwelling in 1890. An important part of the redo was the addition of the marquee. There are few marquees on private homes, but this one is a gem. Assembled of wrought iron, cast iron finials, and glass, it has much in common with the construction used for the conservatory wings of the great Victorian mansions. The marquee blends beautifully with the door grille below. The railings, also attractive, appear to be the work of another designer. Simple, tasteful and practical, they are far less florid. As such, they extend out to just beyond the riser. Each railing requires only one insert into the horizontal surface – the sidewalk. The "C"scrolls against the building strengthen the railings both physically and aesthetically.

MINOR IRONWORK FEATURES

Chapter 8

God is in the details.

Ludwig Mies van der Rohe

Well-designed details in iron frequently elevated some undistinguished buildings into structures of importance and prestige. If an owner placed a beautifully detailed iron lantern at the doorway to his building, the building immediately achieved status. During the Victorian age, even good-looking small features near their front doors added prestige to many houses. Among the more popular details were shoe scrapers.(8-8) Besides being decorative, they were also indispensable adjuncts to tidiness.

To satisfy the demand for decorative items, the foundries and forges made scores of castings and wrought iron details, which were incorporated into buildings and grounds. From hinges to bathtubs, these items were primarily designed to solve functional problems, however many of them were also artistic creations. In the 20th century, universities, churches, banks, and opulent owners wanted distinctive lanterns, knockers, gates, and hardware for their properties. These clients engaged Yellin and other artist-blacksmiths to create hand wrought objects.

And today the renewal of wrought ironwork is underway.

University of Pittsburgh, 8-1
Foster Memorial Library, (1938)
Samuel Yellin, Artist-blacksmith

A wrought iron hinge with ring handle for a large oak door. (Photograph from the Yellin Archives.)

163

2031 Delancey Place, 8-2
Tilden & Register (1916-1925), Architects in 1924

This five story 1860's house was reborn, acquiring its present Regency Revival appearance in 1924. Almost like the arms of a mother holding her infant endearingly, the two wrought iron arms tenderly hold the lantern. The subtle curve of the arms blends beautifully with the rounded iron balcony on the piano nobile. The lantern and balcony are important parts of the ornamentation on this sophisticated, disciplined façade.

James S. Spencer Residence, 8-3
(Now "The Colonial")
1100 Spruce Street
Original Architect unknown
Henry Dandurand Dagit (1865-1929), Façade's Architect

This 1839 residence was expanded and provided with its current façade in 1891, when, in spite of its un-Colonial architecture, it became "The Colonial." At that time, Chicago architect Louis Henry Sullivan was exerting a profound influence on architects nationwide. With the writhing foliage on the façade's stonework, it is clear that architect Dagit was one of the architects whom Sullivan influenced. As Whiffen and Koeper write: It is above all Sullivan's love of ornament and his originality in designing it, that give a subjective stamp to all his designs. His genius escaped the bondage and anonymity of eclecticism, which he deplored. He applied Ruskin's theory of an architecture of encrustation to his own system of brilliant ornament. His earliest designs betray traces of the Gothic Revival and Frank Furness, once briefly his employer.... Sullivan's ornament became the most intricate and seductive in the history of architecture.[1] Dagit's stone carving is definitely Sullivanesque. He designed the iron lanterns flanking the doorway to blend with the stonework. Of course, the ornamented ironwork on the lanterns had to be far more open than the ornament he placed on the stone – without it, the lanterns would have shed little light.

Offices of Mellor and Meigs, 8-4
205 South Juniper Street
Mellor and Meigs, Architects
Samuel Yellin, Artist-blacksmith

This building was originally a mid-19th century carriage house. In 1912, it was extensively remodeled to serve as the office of these talented architects, designers of many of the finest suburban homes in the Philadelphia area. They worked in traditional styles, used ironwork freely and often commissioned Yellin to produce it. Here, for their own offices, they had Yellin create the ironwork. That included the pictured attractive and distinctive door-knocker and hinge on the back door. The main door had a larger and more decorative knocker. It has disap-peared. (The bottom portion of the door is omitted from the photograph. Unfortunately, it has been penetrated with mechanical equipment.)

Henry LaBarre Jayne House, 8-5
1824 Delancey Place
Wilson Eyre and McIlvaine (1912-1930), Architects

In 1895, Eyre designed this handsome, completely new Georgian Revival façade for Jayne. He was refacing an 1857 house, originally owned by James Markoe. The current façade's distinctive character is typical of Eyre's work. The charming and appealing piece of ironwork does more than give the house number. It actually transforms the doorway. Were it not for the ironwork, the dark and cavernous entrance way might seem almost forbidding. But the ironwork adds a light touch and offers a note of welcome to the visitor.

University of Pennsylvania, 8-6
Quadrangle Dormitory
37th and Spruce Streets
Cope and Stewardson, Architects

Strongly influenced by the architecture of Oxford and Cambridge Universities in England, Philadelphia architects Cope and Stewardson designed Penn's Quadrangle and Triangle Dormitories. The first unit was completed in 1895. The architects used their Ox-Bridge style, a type of Jacobean Revival. Since that style employed ironwork freely, there is much of it in these dormitories. Virtually each entrance doorway has a different type of wrought iron lantern. Some are quite handsome. Even the cast iron boots at the bottoms of the downspouts are architectural ironwork.[2]

West Spruce Street Presbyterian Church, 8-7
(Now the Tenth Presbyterian Church)
1700 Spruce Street
John McArthur, Jr., Architect

The architecture of this 1859 church harks back to the Romanesque period in Italy's Lombardy. Similar to many churches in Lombardy, this one is brick. It relies on judiciously placed ornament to give it an architecturally rich appearance. The handsome lanterns and gates are important parts of that ornament. Since it is not mentioned in the early insurance survey, at the Philadelphia Historical Commission, the ironwork may have been added at the turn of the century when architects Frank Miles Day or, later, Edgar V. Seeler altered the church. The pictured decorative iron lantern and gates were artistically designed to harmonize with each other. The design of the gates is noteworthy. Without the band of crosses at their tops, the gates would just be attractive. But with that band of crosses, the gates are outstanding and perfect for the church.

169

Shoe Scraper, 8-8
Rudulph Ellis House
2113 Spruce Street
Furness and Hewitt, Architects

Furness designed this dressed stone house in 1875, early in his career. On it he applied both incised and bas-relief ornament. Following custom for fine houses of the Victorian period, he provided a shoe scraper next to the entrance steps. This distinctive one was probably designed by or at least selected by Furness.

Tree Guard, 8-9
1802 Delancey Street

This floral casting shows how attractive a minor feature such as a tree guard can be.

University City Historical Society, 8-10
Collection at the Firehouse Xarmer's Market
701 South 50th Street

Gravity warm air heating developed during the nineteenth century. Consequently, there was a need for grilles or registers at the heat outlets in the various rooms of a building. Both floor and wall registers were developed, most of them being of cast iron. Many of them were quite stunning. Fortunately, one of the objectives of the University City Historical Society is "to preserve architectural artifacts salvaged from structures no longer standing in University City."[3] The Historical Society has assembled a large number of these registers and housed them in this former firehouse. The photograph shows just a sampling of the collection.

STREET, PARK, & GARDEN FEATURES

Chapter 9

The taste for stag and deer immobilized in iron, sprang up in the late 1840's. From about 1850 on, tidy Victorian lawns were spotted with arrogant, chocolate-covered stags gazing blankly across sunny flower beds, and vast herds of deer roamed through every other phase of Victorian decoration.

Since the English Prince Consort was interested in the greyhound, an enterprising American manufacturer was ready with copies in iron of this graceful hound.

Frances Lichten: Decorative Art of Victoria's Era.

By 1853, the widely read *Godey's Lady's Book* was showing cast iron greyhounds, and Robert Wood's progressive Philadelphia foundry was producing them, and just two years before, in 1851, many well-to-do Americans had visited London's fabulous Crystal Palace. There, for the first time, they saw all sorts of cast iron objects – not only animal replicas but also fountains, benches, lights, signs, drinking fountains, fences, tree grates, urns, and myriad other objects, for both outdoors and indoors. It did not take long for American foundries to produce many of the same things. The various types of cast iron fountains, both naturalistic and sentimental, exhibited in London's Crystal Palace were soon imitated in America.[1] By being cast, they became affordable, and there was a plethora of foundries offering them. Soon, fountains became an imperative for every public park and for the grounds of the wealthy. In public parks and on large estates, the fountains tended to be large. In small gardens, they usually were small.

Typically, in his pattern book *The Model Architect*, Samuel Sloan shows fountains in several of his illustrations. It is amusing that he even shows one in a romantic, naturalistic scene.[2] Other architects published similar works. For example, New England architect Palliser, Palliser & Co. published the book *Model Homes*. It shows a beautiful fountain spouting on the grounds of the residence they designed at Seaside Park, Bridgeport, Connecticut.

Cast iron garden urns quickly became a symbol of gentility. Patterns were most often derived from Gothic and Renaissance garden sources. Iron urns were cheaper than marble ones, yet could have similar highly decorated surfaces. Some were quite successfully painted to look like their stone forebearers and could be set on the smallest garden plot.

New York architect E. C. Hussey authored the book *Home Building, A Reliable Book of Facts Relative to Building, Living, Materials, Costs*. It included a typical foundry advertisement of the time, offering "Fountains, Vases, Statuary, Deer, Dogs, Lions, Settees, Chairs, etc.,"

Numerous such items existed until they were contributed to the drives for scrap metal during the two World Wars.

Cast Iron Gazebo on the grounds of the Charles MacAlaster House, 9-1, facing page
(Now Glen Foerd on the Delaware)
5001 Grant Avenue, at State Road
Architect unknown

During the 19th century, many parks and gardens included gazebos. Wherever possible, they were located at spots commanding interesting views. Frances Lichen writes: By the 1850's every establishment making any pretensions both in city and country had a summerhouse (i.e., gazebo), whether it was made of cast iron, or wooden scrollery, or of natural branches roofed with bark.[3] In 1893, when Robert H. Foerderer bought this 1850's Italianate house and named it Glen Foerd, the gazebo was not there. In 1902, he completely renovated and extended the house. Possibly it was then, when he added the metal features to the garden. As was the fashion, he added a cast iron gazebo, positioning it to command a view of the Delaware River. Furthermore, since metal deer were popular garden features, he added the one pictured, which bears the signature of Wood & Perot. Such deer were usually cast iron or cast bronze and were painted to resemble the live animals.[4] Glen Foerd is now in the public domain.

Metal Deer, 9-2
On the Grounds of the Charles MacAlaster House
5001 Grant Avenue, at State Road
Architect unknown

Cast Iron Fountain in the Athenæum Garden, 9-3
219 South 6th Street

Since the Athenæum is one of Philadelphia's most notable Victorian structures and is the repository of the city's prime collection of Victoriana, it is most appropriate for it to maintain a Victorian garden. Fittingly, for a small urban garden, it is formal and employs a fountain with triple basins as its central feature. All are cast iron.

Cast Iron Urn in the Athenæum Garden, 9-4
219 South 6th Street

"In gardens planted in the 'Grecian' style, stone or composition vases were used at first 'to give a classic and refined aspect to the situation.' By 1850, American foundrymen were ready with cast iron examples. Brimming over with vines and packed with choice flowering plants, iron vases punctuated the grass plats of every park, companioned every well-kept place."[5] The Athenæum's urns, a 1976 gift of Samuel J. Dornsife, are marked "W Adams & Co, 960 N 9-St, Phila." They date from c.1890.

Lamppost, 9-5
1708 Delancey Place

When Philadelphia's streets were lighted by gaslight, there were cast iron lampposts of this general type everywhere. As evening approached, a man called "the Lamp Lighter" walked the streets, carrying a small ladder and a torch with an open flame at the end of a long pipe. He propped his ladder up against the two projecting arms of the lamp post, climbed up a few steps and, using the open flame, lit the gas light. Currently, such lampposts are being cast again, sometimes in aluminum. Today they are usually wired.

Cast Iron Chair, 9-6
Laurel Hill Cemetery
3922 Ridge Avenue

Philadelphia's 1876 Centennial Exposition showed cast iron chairs and benches with ruggedly organic knotted branches or vines, such as grape, honeysuckle, or ivy, twisting and winding themselves into garden furniture. Such furniture was used not only in gardens but also in cemeteries, since Victorian cemeteries, such as Laurel Hell and the Woodlands, served as popular parks.[6] To accommodate the visitors, cemetery plots, frequently fenced in, often included cast iron benches or chairs such as the one pictured.

179

Lamp Post Franklin Institute, 9-7
(Now Atwater Kent Museum)
15 South 7th Street
John Haviland, Architect

The Franklin Institute building, a Greek Revival structure, was based on the Choragic Monument of Thrasyllus, as published in Stuart and Revett's The Antiquities of Athens. The Institute building was erected between 1825 and 1827. The institution was devoted "to providing a practical scientific education for workingmen." The building also housed the nation's first weather bureau and, between 1826 and 1830, the Federal Courts. After the Franklin Institute moved, radio manufacturer A. Atwater Kent purchased the building and converted it into a museum dedicated to the history of Philadelphia. Kent turned it over to the City and it opened in 1939. Fittingly for the building's architecture, the handsome cast iron lanterns flanking the entrance are Classically inspired. Richly ornamented, they contrast pleasantly to the chaste, austere façade.

Gas Jet Eagle, 9-8
Atwater Kent Museum
15 South 7th Street

In 1838, when the Mexican War ended, a great display was mounted by the Philadelphia Gas Works "in honor of victory and peace and the availability of gas for the purpose of ornamental illumination."[7] An account at the time describes the array: The display took place in front of the State House [i. e., Independence Hall] by permission of Councils. By the shaping of gas-pipes and the multiplication of jets from them, figures in fire were made. The Goddess of Peace, seated on a chair holding in her right hand the olive-branch, was the principal figure, nearly thirty feet high. At her feet and by her side were the emblems of commerce, manufactures and agriculture, the anchor, boxes, chests, wheels, the plow, with a ship in the distance. Above all hovered this eagle with wings of fire, surmounted with a halo of stars, and bearing a scroll with the national motto, while below was the simple inscription, "Peace." There were four thousand burners which lighted up this piece.[8] The pictured eagle was found at the Northern Liberties Gas Works, which, in the nineteenth century, had been part of the Philadelphia Gas Works. It may well have been "the eagle with wings of fire" mentioned above, or it hatched from an egg with the same parents!

GOOD IRONWORK PRACTICE

Chapter 10   *Some good, some so-so, and lots plain bad.*

Marcus Valerius

While Valerius was not speaking about ironwork, he could have been. Little has changed in the past 2000 years and a lot of recent ironwork is "plain bad." While some good ironwork is being produced today, it seems the Golden Age has concluded.

Up to this point we've discussed and enjoyed individual examples of good ironwork. Now we must further illuminate their brilliance by exposing the bad – illustrating some mistakes to avoid, using several examples from the past and present.

Aesthetic Considerations

Hopefully this book's analysis of both superior and inferior ironwork will help improve the quality of ironwork being produced currently.

Since Philadelphia tradition dictates that architectural ironwork must first be functional, it should be designed to perform its task well. Only then, after the functional problems have been solved, should it be turned into an art form. Contrast the functional architectural ironwork shown in most of the pictured work with the purely decorative architectural ironwork shown in f-3 and the poorly conceived original architectural ironwork shown in 10-10. While the latter is decorative, it is also intended to be functional; however, it did not work visually.

Ironwork is most striking when it has one design theme fully developed, with everything else subordinated to it. Compare the handsome ironwork in f-1, f-2, f-6, 1-3, 1-8, 5-9, and 6-11 with the functional but less attractive ironwork shown in 10-3.

Architectural ironwork should harmonize with the building to which it is being secured. Note how admirably the rounded balconies shown in figure 7-6 harmonize with the arched openings behind them. Contrast the awkward second floor balcony shown in 10-8 with the excellent one shown in 7-5.

Ironwork should not only be secure but should also look secure. Notice how the Greek key design element in the stair railing shown in 10-5 seems to be sliding down hill. Contrast those Greek keys with those in the splendid stair railing shown in 4-18.

Then there is the issue of consistency in design. Compare the lack of compatibility of the doorway ironwork with the transom ironwork in figure 10-4 as opposed to the far more successful solution to an arched doorway problem shown in 5-11 and 5-17.

Ironwork should relate to the architectural style of its building. Notice how beautifully Yellin's ironwork, shown on f-1, relates to the Gothic architecture of St. Mark's Church. Then perceive how excellently the Grecian fences shown in 2-5, 2-7, and 4-8 harmonize with their Greek Revival buildings. Then consider the ironwork shown in 4-10, 4-14, 4-21, and 4-24. In each instance the ironwork relates admirably to the building's architecture.

If possible, the ironwork should disclose the use of the building or site. Good examples of this are shown in figures 1-6 and 2-1. Photograph 4-19 also illustrates this, but the ironwork may actually predate the present use of the building as a music school. Ironwork design does not have to be elaborate to be effective. 5-6 illustrates an effective gate design, yet it is hardly elaborate. 11-7 and 11-9 illustrate how, by varying the size, spacing, or length of simple iron bars, a railing or fence can be made interesting. 11-4 shows a good contemporary design made from stock modern parts. Although, the gates do not have the subtleties of fine hand crafted wrought iron, they do not cost nearly as much as they would have if they were hand wrought iron.

Technical Considerations

Do not juxtapose two pieces of exterior ironwork directly upon each other. Even if the touching surfaces were painted initially, they will need repainting periodically and there will be no way to repaint them. Ultimately water will get between them, rusting the bottom of the top member and the top of the bottom member. Rusting iron expands, so the joint will open. The rust will wick in more water, accelerating the rusting. In the winter, any water entering that open joint will expand if it freezes, thus further opening the joint. Eventually the iron will disfigure or fail. See 10-6.

Any part of a piece of ironwork which is to be embedded in concrete or masonry must be well protected. Water will eventually get to it. Unless it is well protected, it will rust, expand, and destroy the masonry in time. 10-6 illustrates this as well.

To prevent galvanic corrosion, two dissimilar metals out in the elements must be insulated from each other. Galvanic corrosion occurs when the dissimilar metals are in intimate contact and are in the presence of an electrolyte, such as water containing salt or hydrogen ions. The amount of corrosion will depend on the relative sizes of the metals and where they are on the electrochemical series. The "noble" metal will attack and corrode the "baser" metal. Hence, cast iron, which is "baser," will be assaulted when it is in contact with a more "noble" metal, such as copper. Consequently, if patches must be made, less "noble" terne plate-coated stainless steel is the best material. Also, stainless steel or mild steel can be used for patching cast iron.

Regarding Exterior Railings and Fences

The bottom rail should be 3/8 to 1/2 inch solids.

Channels should never be used. They will collect water.

Tubing should not be used. It will fill with condensate and rust from within.

For long runs of fencing, provide elongated holes on the fence post brackets, the brackets to which the fencing is to be screwed. The screws connecting the fencing to the fence post brackets should be of a metal similar to the fencing. They should be double nutted and not screwed too tightly, thus allowing the fencing to expand and contract in response to temperature changes.

Where there is a danger of the ironwork's being stolen, a bead of weld at the bottom of the screw may thwart the thief's efforts.

Gate posts should be set in cement. Both the iron and the cement should be extended below the frost line. 10-1 shows what can happen when this is not done.

The iron should rest on 1/4-inch iron plates, set on rammed stones.

To keep gate posts properly aligned, it is wise to put a crossbar between them. It should be on a gravel bed and be buried below the frost line. Protect it from rusting, following the recommendations below.

For tall gates, a top crossbar is also recommended, but it must be 84 inches or more above the grade.

If the gate swings on male members, inserted into female members on the gatepost, beads of weld on the ends of the male members may prevent the disappearance of the gate.

Restoration and Maintenance of Ironwork

When restoring ironwork, it is wise to use preservation architects or conservators to first assess the condition. If the work is to be contracted, they can prepare contract documents.

Prior to the start of any work, it is important to check with the local building department, any environmental protection agencies, and the historical or landmark commission. Be sure that the proposed work violates no regulations.

Before commissioning artisans to make repairs, examine some of their previous restorations. Ascertain whether their type of technology is apropos to subject project.

For accomplishing the actual work, no one but an artisan should be used to do any necessary cutting and fitting, tapping and finishing.

CAUTION! Much iron maintenance work is dangerous and should be done only by qualified workers with suitable protective equipment. One example of the danger is paint removal by sand blasting. It creates highly toxic dust, so it is MANDATORY that operatives be properly protected from this toxic dust.

An iron object may be badly rusted. The rusting may have resulted from the presence of water, salt air, sea water, acids, acid rain, and other air pollutants. If the iron had crevices which trapped and held liquid corrosive elements, the rust may be especially bad. The rusted surfaces were porous, so they acted as reservoirs for liquids. This causes further rusting.

Before actual restoration, ALL rust and paint must be removed. Chip away any loose paint or rust. Then, if local regulations permit it, blast with dry grit using blasting pressure no higher than 80 to 100 pounds per square inch and 70-100 mesh particles. If local regulations do not permit blasting or if the member is excessively thin, then use a wire brush. In any event, if any repairs are to be made, it is important to get down to bright metal.

NO type of WET blasting is appropriate. It will rust the iron immediately!

Repair and Maintenance of Cast Iron

Once an iron casting is clean, various imperfections may be revealed. Some may even go back to the original manufacture of the casting. Discoveries may include cracks, air holes, cinders, or cold shuts – the latter caused by interrupted pouring or "freezing" of the surface during casting. Occasionally, old castings are excessively brittle. Sometimes they have impact damage, structural failure, broken joints, damaged connections, missing elements, or loss of anchorage in masonry.

Non-structural small cracks and holes can be filled with epoxy steel. Although cast iron is difficult to weld, it can be welded with a pure nickel rod. All nickel welds should be peened with a chipping hammer to relieve built-up internal stresses. Such stresses may cause under-bed cracking or breaking of the cast iron at the interface with the nickel.

Importantly, welding should NEVER be used for cast iron STRUCTURAL members. Defective structural members MUST be replaced. Also, replace any cast iron structural members found to be less than 3/8 inch thick with steel.

If missing portions of a casting are to be supplied, a carefully prepared pattern must be produced. The pattern's use is explained above in the chapter on cast ironwork. Remember, iron shrinks 1/8 inch per foot as it changes from molten metal to a solid. To allow for the shrinkage of the molten metal as it cools, the pattern must be slightly enlarged from the desired size of the casting.

To save time and expense, an existing similar casting can be used as a pattern. However the resulting new casting will be slightly smaller than the original due to the shrinkage mentioned above.

Replacement castings can be of aluminum, which was not available during the cast iron period. It will not rust; however, to prevent electrolytic action, aluminum must be insulated from the iron. Spar varnish is good for that.

Only stainless steel pins or fasteners should be used in reassembling old units or adding new ones.

Repair and Maintenance of Wrought Iron

If repairs are to be made, let the artisans submit samples of their work. Make sure that they are experienced in the type of technology needed for your project. Once approved, they should be employed to do any necessary cutting, fitting, tapping and finishing.

As with cast iron, after all rust and loose paint have been removed, there should be a detailed condition assessment of the piece.

For protecting interior wrought iron, varnish is preferable to paint. However, on the interior, a better system for revealing the evidence of the ironsmith's handiwork is a thin coat of wax, mixed with a little boiled linseed oil. If this is rubbed on the iron periodically, it will prevent rust and, at the same time, allow the ironsmith's hammer marks to show.

Some museum conservators are using a 10% solution of tannic acid for protecting ironwork—both cast and wrought. The solution is composed of tannic acid, deionized or distilled water, ethanol, and dilute phosphoric acid. It produces a blue-black finish. It is only to be used for ironwork which is to remain indoors, with a controlled environment. The system is fully described in CCI Notes 9/5, published by the Canadian Conservation Institute, 1030 Innes Road, Ottawa, Ontario K1A0M5, Canada.

Rust-Proofing Ironwork

Ironwork on the exterior stands up best if it is rustproofed with a phosphate plating. Better yet, especially at the seashore, it should be plated with zinc or hot dip galvanized and a phosphate plating prior to painting. The Navy uses the latter process.

After the ironwork has been rust proofed, it should be painted with a rust-inhibitive paint.

Painting Existing Exterior Ironwork

Once any repairs have been made and any replacements added, all exterior ironwork should be painted immediately to prevent rusting.

Regardless of which paint system is used, the surfaces must be properly prepared. The ironwork must be clean, free of rust, scale, grease, or oil. Poorly prepared surfaces will not retain even the best paint.

Never paint on a wet or damp surface.

Never paint during a fog, mist or rain, or when the relative humidity is above 80%.

Never paint if the temperature is expected to fall below 50 degrees° F. within 24 hours.

Preferably, do not paint ironwork in direct sunlight. The paint dries too quickly.

First, cover the metal with a quality rust inhibitive metal primer.
Red lead was the traditional primer. It is tough, elastic, and impervious to water. However, it contains heavy metal compounds and is toxic, as is zinc chromate, another good primer, so now both of them are prohibited in most areas. (Some areas do allow them to be used for industrial purposes, such as tanks.)

Today alkyd or acrylic primers have replaced them. While these dry faster, their effective life is shorter. Alkyd rust-inhibitive primers contain pigments such as iron oxide, zinc oxide, and zinc phosphate. Such primers are suitable for replacement parts and for cleaned, previously painted surfaces. One coat, or better yet two, should be used. Follow them with finish coats of alkyd enamel or, for better color and gloss retention, silicone alkyd. Make sure that the finish paint contains rust inhibitors, fungicides, and ultra-violet blockers.

For longer protection, zinc-rich primers containing zinc dust can be used. However, such primers can be used only on new sand blasted pieces, shop cleaned to a "bare white" condition.

Never use water based latex house paints as primers on bare iron. They will cause immediate rust.

The primer coats should be followed with even, not too thick, finish coats which can range from matte to glossy.

For cast iron, the better available paint system is a two part epoxy primer, followed by a polyurethane finish coat. However, this paint system is expensive and is difficult for non-professionals to apply.

While most ironwork is painted black, black tends to mask details. Shadows, which help define depth, tend to disappear. Painting ironwork sensitively, with colors, can enhance its appearance. An examples of this is shown in 2-4, 3-7, and 4-13.

There is a system of painting exterior hand wrought ironwork which favors depth definition and hammer mark display. First, get the ironwork to be absolutely clean. Then apply a two-coat epoxy varnish.

Although other manufacturers have similar paint systems, Sherwin-Williams's systems are cited below. This is because they have outlets everywhere. They suggest the following specifications for painting exterior ironwork:[1]

1. On new exterior ironwork or old exterior ironwork which is dry and in sound condition and from which ALL loose paint and rust have been removed, cover the entire piece with a coat of DTM Acrylic Primmer/Finish and allow at least a day for that to dry.

2. Next, apply two coats of DTM Acrylic Coating, either gloss or semi-gloss.

3. Allow at least a day for each coat to dry before recoating.

A better, longer lasting system follows. However, it is more expensive:

1. On new exterior ironwork or old exterior ironwork which is dry and in sound condition and from which ALL paint and rust have been removed, cover the entire piece with one coat of epoxy primer. (Sherwin-Williams Epolon II Rust-Inhibitive Primer)

2. Over the primer, apply two coats of aliphatic polyurethane paint. (Polylon 1900. It is available in a wide variety of colors.)

3. Give each coat at least two or better three days to dry before applying the next coat.

If part of a railing is to be set in cement, then that part of the unit should be treated as follows:

1. Make sure that the entire portion of new exterior ironwork, or old exterior ironwork which is to be encased in cement is dry and in sound condition and free of ALL rust and previous paint.

2. Apply a coat of an epoxy primer to the ironwork. (Sherwin-Williams Epolon II Rust-Inhibitive Primer)

3. Cover the portion of the ironwork which is to be buried with a second coat, that coat to be a coal tar epoxy. (Sherwin-Williams Hi-Mil Sher-Tar, B-69-B-40)

4. Allow 10 to 14 days for the coal tar epoxy to cure.

5. Set the ironwork in the hole.

6. Pour quick setting hydraulic cement around the buried piece of iron. Mound it up to shed water. Remember that the cement is not waterproof and must be sealed periodically.

7. An industrial flexible epoxy sealant is an alternative. It has the advantage of being waterproof and slightly flexible — allowing for thermal expansion of the iron.

Follow one of the above paint systems for those portions of the unit which will be exposed to the elements.

If a railing is to be set in stonework, (e.g., marble, granite, brownstone, etc.) drill a hole in the masonry unit and follow the above technique. Be sure to set it at least 4″ back from all edges, so that the lever action of the pull on the stone by those using the railing will not break the stone.

At least the part of the unit which will be buried should rust-proofed.

Better yet, the entire unit should be rust-proofed.

After the ironwork is set, then one of the above paint systems should be followed for those portions of the unit which will be exposed to the elements.

Some years ago the Friends of Cast Iron Architecture published a digest of the specification used for maintenance of the cast iron dome of the United States Capitol. Since this may be helpful to those preserving cast iron façades and structures, essential elements of that digest are included below:

1. Remove all foreign matter.
2. Using chipping hammers and wire-brushes, carefully remove all loose paint and all rusted and scaling metal from the iron surface. Wire-brush all rusted and scaling spots and clean all areas where the old paint is not scaling.
3. Replace any corroded screws, bolts or connecting members.
4. Prior to painting, caulk all joints and points where water could enter.
5. Reprime all bare metal immediately. Use a basic, alkyd type, ready mixed paint–one conforming to Government specifications for this type of paint.
6. After the primer is thoroughly dry, apply a top coat of the color desired. Again alkyd based, it should conform to Government specifications for this type of paint.

Galvanizing

Galvanizing is the process of coating ironwork with zinc, a technique that give ironwork great protection from corrosion. Galvanizing is beyond the scope of this discussion, however it is fully explained in publications by the: American Galvanizers Association, 6881 South Holly Circle, Englewood, CO 80112. 1-800-HOT-SPEC.

Maintenance Manuals

Proper maintenance of ironwork is covered more fully and especially well in the following works, among others:

New Edge of the Anvil by Jack Andrews. This covers all aspects of wrought iron smithing. Skipjack Press, Ocean Pines, MD 21811. Updated in 1994.

The following two publications are published by the U. S. Department of the Interior, National Park Service, Cultural Resources, Preservation Assistance Division. They are for sale by the Superintendent of Documents, U. S. Government Printing Office, Washington, DC 20402-9328:

The Maintenance and Repair of Architectural Cast Iron, by John G. Waite, with Historical Overview by Margot Gayle. Preservation Brief #27. 1991

Metals in America's Historic Building, by Margot Gayle, David W. Look, and John G. Waite. This work covers various metals and is particularly informative on cast iron. Updated in 1992.

Organizations

The following organizations are excellent sources of information and creators of ironwork:

*Artist-Blacksmith's Association of North America, (ABANA), PO Box 816, Farmington, GA 30638. www.abana.org 706-310-1030.

*National Ornamental & Miscellanious Metals Association, (NOMMA), 804 Main Stree, Suite F, Forest park, GA 30297 404-363-4009.

Leaning Fence, 10-1

Here an historic fence in upstate Pennsylvania suffers from the fact that its foundation was not carried down below the frost line. Over the years, the alternate freezing and thawing of the soil undermined the fence's foundations. Consequently, the fence shifted. (Author's Photograph)

J. M. Gibbon House, 10-2
1608 Spruce Street
Prescott A. Hopkins (fl. 1904 - 1908), Architect for the Refacing

The Gibbon house was completely refaced in 1906. The basically simple but sophisticated railing belongs to the Arts and Crafts period. Note the subtle refinement contributed by the upward bends at both ends of the top rails. The judicious placement of a series of "C" scroll castings has converted the railing into a delicate, decorative embellishment to the entrance of the house. However, the "C" scrolls are more than decoration. Functionally, they brace the railing. Attractive as it is, the railing embodies an error, the baluster was set too close to the edge of the stone. Consequently, the lever action of people using the railing broke the stone.

1624 Spruce Street, 10-3
Architect unknown

This rendition of the Roman rinceau design is far leaner than many castings of this design. The attempt to adapt the stock rectangular casting to the segmental arched opening is quite unsuccessful. Thin as the rinceau is, it is plump in comparison to the two emaciated, out-of-scale elongated "S" scrolls perched uneasily above the rectangular casting.

J. P. Keating Residence, 10-4
322 South 16th Street
Lindley Johnson (1854-1937), 1905 Architect

This house received its Regency façade in 1905. Its later occupant, Andrew N. Farnese, Esq., had this interesting contemporary doorway grille installed below the lintel. The ironworker incorporated the aristocratic "Farnese" family name above the door and the family's coat of arms on the door itself. Then he deftly cut the mail slot into the bottom rail of the door. Unfortunately the fanlight transom, remaining from the previous Regency doorway, is hardly compatible.

191

1718 Pine Street, 10-5
Architect unknown

This late Greek Revival house was built c.1851 by developer McCray. The Greek key design of its stair railing works admirably on the platform. When it is applied to the steps, however, it produces an unsatisfactory result. Because it was not adapted to the slope, it seems to be sliding down hill. Contrast this stair rail with those shown on the more successful railings shown in figures 4-18, 4-26, and 4-29.

1912 Spruce Street, 10-6
Architect unknown

This is one of a group of three Italianate houses built c.1855. The ironworker that produced this railing, decades ago, made a number of critical mistakes: For the top rail, he used two pieces of iron, bedding one directly on the other. Thus, it became impossible to paint the top of the bottom piece or the bottom of the top piece. Eventually water got in between them and both pieces rusted. This expanded the iron, so the two pieces started to pry themselves apart. The rust wicked in still more water, causing further rusting. During the winter, water entered and expanded as it froze, further prying the members apart. As the iron continued to rust, it expanded further. Eventually the two pieces pried themselves fully loose from each other. He placed the newel too close to the edge of the stone. The lever action of people using the rail, started to expand the hole in the stone and crack it. Water entered the hole and the crack and expanded as it froze. This put further pressure on the stone. Before he lodged the iron newels into the stone, the ironworker did not rustproof them. Eventually water got to the buried portions and they rusted. They expanded as they rusted. That expansion, coupled with the expansion of entering water, tended to further crack the stone. Finally, the unsupported newel broke off.

2010 Spruce Street, 10-7
Architect unknown

Built c. 1860, this Second Empire style house is part of the 2006-2012 group of brownstones. The decorative rectangular design of this cast window grille appears in the Robert Wood and later, Wood & Perot, catalogs. It was so popular that it was imitated many times. Here the various features have clear, crisp outlines. Many of the other renditions of this pattern are far cruder. While the pattern's rendition is clear and crisp, it is a total misfit here. It belongs in a rectangular opening. The fill in above the pattern, up to the arch, is singularly discordant.

1723 Spruce Street, 10-8
Architect unknown

This 1893 Jacobean Revival style façade on an 1860's house is dominated by its two-story bay. The relationship of the ironwork on the two balconies, to the curved bay, provides an interesting contrast. The fourth floor balcony is successful. It echoes the curved wall. Functionally, the second floor balcony provides maximum sitting space. Aesthetically, that balcony and its railing suffer from their complete lack of relationship to the curved wall. Contrast the later with the aesthetically pleasing solution to a similar situation, the balcony shown on 7-5.

UNIQUE IRONWORK SOLUTIONS

Chapter 11

Daffy's, 11-1
1700 Chestnut Street
Jacobs/Wypers, Architects
Bella Abdallah, Gate designer
Richard R. Pucci, Ironworker

These contemporary gates get their elegance from the curved line of their tops – the converse of the arch above. Beyond that, the use of iron bars of different weights, helps the design. The thinner, wavy rods contrast pleasantly with the stronger straight ones. The little bronze balls atop the more slender rods, add a bit of icing to the cake. Hopefully, the two different metals are insulated from each other, to avoid electrolytic action.

2046 Ranstead Street, 11-2
Alan J. Feltoon, A.I.A., (1952-) Architect
Christopher T. Ray, (1937-2000), Artist-blacksmith

This attractive, contemporary gate, composed of stock parts, gets its distinction from good design. While not great hand wrought iron-work, it is certainly far more handsome than most current gates.

330 South Front Street, 11-3
The Iron Men (1969-), Artist-blacksmiths

When Nic and Eileen East, of The Iron Men, designed this ironwork, they related it carefully to the axis of the bay above. Probably the arches and the zigzags at the top of the screen had to be especially fabricated. However, for the most part, this piece of ironwork is an assemblage of stock material. The result is certainly quite handsome.

199

738 Manning Street, 11-4
Ironworker unknown

While certainly not masterpieces of ironwork, these contemporary gates are good looking, simple, and made of stock parts. The design starts with the blank circular plates needed for the lock and security. Then, with concentric bars, the design expands on the circular theme. Welded to the vertical bars, the concentric bars not only harmonize with the blank plates but they also brace the gates. Finally, the borders, top and bottom, echo the circles with a series of rings.

Eugene's, 11-5
1527 South Street
Ironworker unknown

This 1860's house became a store in about 1880. For security, the current shopkeeper could have installed a forbidding, unsightly jalousie. Instead, he had an artist ironworker produce this interesting composition. Although it protects the property, it also makes the shop more aesthetically desirable. While a number of the members had to be bent, much of the unit is formed of stock parts. The result is both unusual and artistic.

1931 Manning Street, 11-6
Architect and ironworker unknown

This c.1910 Georgian Revival building is currently a residence. Originally, it probably was a carriage house. Its architect took great pains to create a handsome structure. He used the exposed beam to support the outer visible wythe of brickwork above the carriage door. Undoubtedly he placed additional beams behind it to support the hidden wythes of brickwork. The architect wanted to be sure that all the beams would act in unison, hence the bolts. Instead of simply inserting the bolts through the assembly indiscriminately, he turned the bolts into decorative features. Thus, he converted a functional necessity into an artistic achievement.

Weightman Building, 11-7
Northeast corner, 22nd and Chestnut Streets
Ironworker unknown

This fence surrounds the grounds of a former church, which has been converted into an office building. The simple, economical, and contemporary fence can be duplicated easily. It looks so much better than a standard, unimaginative fence.

1545 South Street, 11-8
Ironworker unknown

Although hardly a showpiece of the ironworker's art, this contemporary gate demonstrates how even a simple design, economically produced, can be made more attractive.

Donovan Residence, 11-9
(Now the Saffron House Restaurant)
121 South 19th Street
Ironworker unknown

This 1890s Queen Anne brick and brownstone house has a number of handsome pressed metal bays. Decades after the house was built, the railings were added by the late Beryl Price (1910-1978), the architect who lived in the house for many years. While his design is of the Modern School, it harmonizes with the house. The two railings are chaste, unique, and handsome. By rhythmically contrasting rods of different sizes, Price cleverly and simply created the two interesting pieces of ironwork. He installed large brass balls as finials, but they were stolen. The pictured finials are replacements by later occupants. These railings serve two functions: they help people up the step, and they keep passers-by from tripping over the original low step that encroaches on the sidewalk. Being only a single step, it could easily be missed.

John C. Bullitt House, 11-10, *facing page 11-11*
125 South 22nd Street
George Watson Hewitt and William D. Hewitt, Original Architects
Edward B. Bronstein, A.I.A. (1944-), Restoration Architect
Greg Leavitt (1947-), Artist-Blacksmith

This large and impressive former residence was built for Bullitt, a prominent attorney in the year 1886. Later, it served architect Frank Furness as his office when the great Louis Henry Sullivan (1856-1924) worked for him, before he, Sullivan, migrated to Chicago. The present owners of the building restored it carefully. Historically, there probably was a small front garden, with a fence where the present one is. However, the fence was lost and there was no record of what it had been. Following the Secretary of the Interior's Standards recommendation, a new design was created which took its cue from the historic second floor ironwork but was not a fake Hewitt creation. It is a handsome contemporary fence that relates beautifully to the historic dwelling. (See page xii.) The handsome original hinges on the entrance door are a good introduction to the attractive interiors beyond.

122 Spruce Street, 11-12
Christopher T. Ray, Artist-blacksmith

This is a remarkable example of present day, artistic hand wrought ironwork. The free-flowing naturalistic pieces of metal are not only protective, but they do an admirable job of softening the hard lines of this contemporary house. They almost seem to be moving with the breeze. Although this gate and the gate on the facing page are contemporary wrought ironwork, the sensuous curves have something of an Art Nouveau character.[1]

"Wissahickon Valley Gate," 11-13
Chestnut Park
17th and Chestnut Streets
Delta Group (1972-), Landscape Architects
Christopher T. Ray, Artist-blacksmith

The obituary for the late Christoper T. Ray stated that he considered this gate to be his Masterpiece – and a masterpiece it is. It is a fitting grand finale to this work. With its natural, floral forms, the gate is certainly an appropriate adjunct to a garden. Curves notwithstanding, it fits in beautifully within its rectangular frame. While functionally it is a gate, it certainly is a work of art and a testimony to the spirit of iron.

LIST OF PHOTOGRAPHS

5. Gates and Doors

6. Window and Door Grilles

NOTES

Forword

1. Dimitri Gerakaris, editor: "Samuel Yellin, Metalworker," Anvil's Ring Magazine; Summer,1982.
2. Church records.
3. Philip B. Wallace, *Colonial Ironwork in Old Philadelphia*. (New York: Architectural Book Publishing Co., Inc., 1930).
4. Baldwin and Thomas: *Gazetteer*, p. 917.
5. *Wealth and Biography of the Wealthy Citizens of Philadelphia*, pp. 1-23.
6. Ralph Chiumenti, *Cast Iron Architecture in Philadelphia*. (New York: Friends of Cast-Iron Architecture, 1976) pp. 1-7.
7. Edward and Elizabeth Waugh, *The South Builds*. (Chapel Hill: University of South Carolina Press, 1960) p. 17.
8. Robert P. Winthrop, *Cast and Wrought, the Architectural Metalwork of Richmond, Virginia*. (Richmond: Valentine Museum, 1980) p. 31.
9. Jack Andrews, *Samuel Yellin, Metalworker*. (Ocean Pines, MD: Skipjack Press, 2000), Index pages 1 to 11.
10. Frances Lichten, *Decorative Art of Victoria's Era*. (New York: Charles Scribner's Sons, 1950), p. 104.
11. Ann M. Masson and Lydia J. Owen, *Cast Iron and the Crescent City*. (New Orleans, LA: Gallier House, 1975), p. 4.
12. Italo William Ricciuti, *New Orleans and Its Environs: the Domestic Architecture, 1727-1870*. (New York: William Heilburn, Inc., 1938), p. 11.
13. Margot Gayle and David W. Look, A *Historical Survey of Metals, in Metals in America's Historic Buildings*. (Washington: U.S. Department of the Interior, Heritage Conservation and Recreation Service, 1980), p. 67.
14. Ann M. Masson, and Lydia J. Owen, *Cast Iron and the Crescent City*. (New Orleans, LA, Gallier House, 1975), pp. 18, 19.

1. Wrought Ironwork

1. Samuel Yellin, *Iron in Art*. (Encyclopedia Britannica, 14th edition, 1940) volume 12.
2. Nathaniel Lloyd, *History of the English House*. (New York: William Helburn, Inc., 1931) p. 464.
3. Samuel Yellin, *Iron in Art*. (Encyclopedia Brittanica, 14th edition, 1940) volume 12.
4. *Samuel Yellin: Poet of Iron*. Quoted by Fullerton Waldo in The Outlook, December 31, 1924.
5. The firm was Mellor, Meigs and Howe from 1916 to 1926.
6. Information supplied by Mr. Galen Horst-Martz, Executive Director, Germantown Mennonite Historic Trust.
7. Gerald K. Geerlings, *Wrought Iron in Architecture*. (New York: Charles Scribner's Sons, 1929) p.142.
8. Quoted in the "Anvil's Ring," Summer 1982. Edited by Dimitri Gerakaris.
9. The dates of the various examples of Yellin's work are established in the Yellin Job Cards which Jack Andrews includes in his monograph, *Samuel Yellin, Metalworker*.

2. Cast Ironwork

1. Ralph Chiumenti, *Cast Iron Architecture in Philadelphia*. (New York: Friends of Cast-Iron Architecture, 1976).
2. Edward Kirk et al, *The Founding of Metals*, 5th edition. (New York: David Williams, 1855).
3. Daniel D. Badger, *Badger's Illustrated Catalogue of Cast Iron Architecture*. (New York: 1865, Dover reprint, 1981).
4. Elizabeth M. Geffen, *Industrial Development and Social Crisis 1841-1854 in Philadelphia, A 300 Year History*, Russell F. Weigley, editor. (New York: W. W. Norton & Co., 1982) p. 327.
5. *The Manufactories and Manufacturers of Pennsylvania of the Nineteenth Century*. (Philadelphia: Galaxy Publishing Co., 1875).
6. Frances Lichten, *Decorative Art of Victoria's Era*. (New York: Charles Scribner's Sons, 1950) p.104.
7. Margot Gayle and David W. Look, A *Historical Survey of Metals, in Metals in America's Historic Buildings*. (Washington: U.S. Department of the Interior, Heritage Conservation and Recreation Service, 1980) p. 73.
8. Robert P Winthrop, *Cast and Wrought, the Architectural Metalwork of Richmond, Virginia*. (Richmond: Valentine Museum, 1980) p. 31.

9. Agnes Addison Gilchrist, *William Strickland, Architect and Engineer, 1788-1854.* (Philadelphia: University of Pennsylvania Press, 1950) pp. 73 -76.
10. Letter to the author from Robert W. Tomlinson, R.A., City Hall Project Architect, August 24, 1993.
11. Insurance survey of 12/1/1885 by Edwin Raf Snyder. At the Philadelphia Historical Commission.
12. Alexander Speltz, *The Styles of Ornament.* (New York: Dover reprint, 1959) p. 48, pl. 18.
13. James F. O'Gorman, *The Architecture of Frank Furness.* (Philadelphia: Philadelphia Museum of Art, 1973) pp. 164 - 171.

3. Cast Iron Façades

1. James Marston Fitch, *American Building,* 2nd edition. (New York: Schocken Books, 1973) p. 122.
2. Turpin C. Bannister, Bogardus Revisited, Part I: The Iron Fronts, in the "Journal of the Society of Architectural Historians," XV, 4, p.12 - 22.
3. James Bogardus, *Cast Iron Buildings: Their Construction and Advantages.* (New York: James Bogardus, 1858).
4. The Architectural Review and American Builders' Journal, March 1870.
5. Ralph Chiumenti, *Cast Iron Architecture in Philadelphia.* (New York: Friends of Cast Iron Architecture, 1976) p. 1.
6. Margot Gayle and David W. Look, *A Historical Survey of Metals,* in Metals in America's Historic Buildings. (Washington: U.S. Department of the Interior, Heritage Conservation and Recreation Service, 1980) pp. 42 - 53.
7. Ralph Chiumenti, *Cast Iron Architecture in Philadelphia.* p. 6.
8. Ann M. Masson & Lydia: *Owen Cast Iron and the Crescent City.* (New Orleans: Gallier House, 1975) p.3.
9. Margot Gayle, *Baltimore and Its Cast-Iron Architecture Foreword to Baltimore's Cast-Iron Buildings & Architectural Ironwork.* (Centerville, MD: Tidewater Publisher, 1991) p. vii.
10. J. Scott Howell: *The Founder's Art in Baltimore's Cast-Iron Buildings & Architectural Ironwork.* p. 13.
11. Philip W. Bishop, *The Beginnings of Cheap Steel.* (Washington: contributions from the Museum of History and Technology: Papers, Smithsonian Institution, 1959).
12. Marcus Whiffen and Frederick Koeper: *American Architecture, 1607-1976.* (London: Routledge & Kegan Paul, 1981) p. 238.
13. David G. Wright, *The Sun Iron Building in Baltimore's Cast-Iron Buildings & Architectural Ironwork.* p. 32.
14. An Oram & Co. drawing, entitled Iron Store Front was published in *The Architectural Review and Builders' Journal,* Vol. 11. (March 1870) facing page 510. It appears to be the Smythe Stores. The missing tooth is shown in photos at the Historical Commission.
15. Insurance survey by Louis Moore, May 5, 1873.
16. Insurance surveys at the Philadelphia Historical Commission.
17. John C Waite, *The Maintenance and Repair of Architectural Cast Iron.* (Washington, National Park Service's Preservation Brief #27, 1992) p.2.
18. Newspaper accounts from the Philadelphia Public Ledger, 1851.
19. Insurance survey by D. R. Knight, October 22, 1851.25. Chiumenti: ibid. p.3.
20. Façade easement documents at the Philadelphia Historical Commission.
21. *1896 Hexamer & Son Insurance Maps of Philadelphia,* Volume II. This shows a 7-story building at 718 Arch St.
22. Richard Webster, *Philadelphia Preserved: Catalog of the Historic American Buildings Survey.* (Philadelphia: Temple University Press, 1976) pp. 175-176.
23. Samuel Sloan, *The Model Architect, an architectural pattern book.* (Philadelphia: E.S. Jones & Co., 1852. Dover reprint, 1980).
24. Letter to the author from Ray K. Metzker, owner, received August 10, 1994.
25. Ralph Chiumenti, ibid., p. 3.
26. Philadelphia Inquirer, June 10, 1879 and Real Estate Record and Builder's Guide, October 10, 1900 (Vol. 15) p. 649.
26. John C. Waite, *The Maintenance and Repair of Architectural Cast Iron,* (Washington: National Park Service's Preservation Brief #27, 1992) p. 2.
27. Marcus Whiffen, *American Architecture Since 1780.* (Cambridge, MA: MIT Press, 1969) p. 184.

4. Fences and Railings

1. Samuel Sloan, *The Model Architect, an architectural pattern book.* (Philadelphia: E.S. Jones & Co., 1852). Dover reprint as Sloan's Victorian Buildings, 1980, pp. 41-42.
2. Wood and Perot, *Portfolio of Original Designs of Iron Railings, Verandas, Settees, Chairs, Tables, and Other Ornamental Ironwork.* (Philadelphia, foundry catalog, 1858).

3. James R. Sullivan, *Historic Grounds Report*. (Part I) on The State House Yard, (Philadelphia: Independence National Historical Park) pp. 14, 15; illustration 15.

4. Margot Gayle and David W. Look, *A Historical Survey of Metals, in Metals in America's Historic Buildings* (Washington: U. S. Department of the Interior, National Park Service, 1992.) p. 67, figure 89.

5. Ann M. Masson and Lydia J Owen, *Cast Iron and the Crescent City*. (New Orleans, LA; Gallier House, 1975) p. 25.

6. J. B. Wickersham, *A New Phase in the Iron Manufacture. Important Inventions and Improvements; Historical Sketch of Iron; Descriptive Catalogue of the Manufactures of the New York Wire Railing Company*. Reprinted by the Athenæum of Philadelphia as Victorian Ironwork: A Catalogue by J. B. Wickersham, with a new historical introduction by Margot Gayle, 1977.

7. Margot Gayle and David W. Look, *A Historical Survey of Metals, in Metals in America's Historic Buildings*. ibid., p.68.

8. Robert J. Joy, M.D.: Yellow Jack, a lecture by Dr. Joy, Professor and Chairman, Medical History Section, Uniformed Services, University of the Health Sciences. The lecture was delivered to the Fellows of the College of Physicians of Philadelphia and the Library Company of Philadelphia, October 27, 1993.

9. Report to the Woodlands Cemetery Co. of the Committee to Visit Mt. Auburn. Penned by authors Eli Kirk Price and Philip M Price. Phila., February 17, 1843. Incorporated in The Charter, By-laws and Regulations of the Woodlands Cemetery Company, with a List of the Lot-holders to March 1, 1868. (Philadelphia: Collins Printer, 1868) pp. 14, 15, 21. Tim Long's masters thesis, The Woodlands. In the Fine Arts Library at the University of Pennsylvania.

10. George Thomas, in Pennsylvania Historic Resource Survey.

11. Charles Dickens, American Notes.

12. George B. Tatum, *Penn's Great Town*. (Philadelphia: University of Pennsylvania Press, 1961) p. 69.

13. National Register of Historic Places nomination by Delaware Valley Regional Planning Commission.

14. Otto Sperr, *A Brief History of 1920 Spruce*.

15. John Harris and Jill Lever, *Illustrated Glossary of Architecture, 850-1830*. (London: Faber and Faber, 1966) Plate 210.

16. Pennsylvania Historic Resource Survey.

17. Philadelphia Historical Commission's files: including insurance surveys, brief of title, newspaper clippings, old photos, research summaries, and the 1892 year book of the Bourse.

18. Philadelphia Historical Commission's files: including insurance surveys, brief of title, newspaper clippings, old photos, and research summaries.

5. Gates and Doors

1. Arthur E. Elsen, *Rodin*. (Garden City, NY: Doubleday & Co., 1963) p.221.

2. Philadelphia Art Jury submission, file 1892. Committee meeting minutes, April 7, 1926.

3. Theo B. White, *Paul Philippe Cret*. (Philadelphia: The Art Alliance Press, 1973) p.34.

4. Alexander Speltz: *The Styles of Ornament*. ibid. Gateway on plate 280.

5. Francis James Dallet, *An Architectural View of Washington Square*. (Philadelphia: 1968) pp. 28-31.

6. Pennsylvania Historic Resources Survey.

7. Alexander Speltz, *The Styles of Ornament*. Door to the tabernacle in the Church of St. Gereon, Cologne (New York: Dover reprint, 1959) Plate 238.

8. Alexander Speltz, *The Styles of Ornament*. ibid.

9. American Architect and Building News (October 14, 1876).

10. Theo B White, ibid., plates 11, 21, 24.

11. Files of the Philadelphia Historical Commission.

6. Window and Door Grilles

1. Margot Gayle, David Look, and John Waite, *Metals in America's Historic Buildings*. (Washington: Heritage Conservation and Recreation Service, 1980) p. 63.

2. Richard Glazier, *A Manual of Historic Ornament*, 4th edition. (New York: Van Norstrand Reinhold Co., 1983) pp.24, 25, pl. 8, 9.

3. Elizabeth Biddle Yarnall, *Addison Hutton*. (Philadelphia: Art Alliance Press, 1974) fig. 6.

4. Alexander Speltz: ibid., p. 52, and pl. 21.

5. James F. O'Gorman, *The Architecture of Frank Furness*. (Philadelphia: Philadelphia 96. Museum of Art, 1973) p.173.

6. Files of Philadelphia Historical Commission.

7. Alexander Speltz, ibid., p. 80, pl. 38.

8. Files of the Philadelphia Historical Commission.

9. Alexander Speltz, ibid., p. 496, pl. 307.

10. George Thomas, Pennsylvania Historic Resources Survey.
11. Pennsylvania Inventory of Historic Places.
12. Gerald K. Geerlings, *Wrought Iron in Architecture*. (New York: Dover reprint, 1983) p. 119, fig. 157.
13. Alexander Speltz, *The Styles of Ornament*. (New York: Dover reprint, 1959) p. 375, pl. 226.
14. James C. Massey, *Frank Furness in the 1870's*. (Charette, January, 1963 issue) p.16.
14. Janis E. Newell, St. Anthony's Clubhouse, Files of the Philadelphia Historical Commission.
15. James F. O'Gorman, *The Architecture of Frank Furness*. ibid. pp. 98, 99.

7. Minor Strcutures

1. Ann M. Masson and Lydia J Owen, *Cast Iron and the Crescent City*. (New Orleans, LA: Gallier House, 1975) p. 31.
2. E. Graeme Robertson and Joan Robertson, *Cast Iron Decoration*. (New York: Thames & Hudson, Inc., 1994), pp. 263-264.
3. Numerous newspaper clippings at the Philadelphia Historical Commission.
4. Pennsylvania Historic Resources Survey.
5. Numerous newspaper clippings at the Philadelphia Historical Commission.
6. F. R. Yerbury, *Georgian Details of Domestic Architecture*. (Boston and New York: Houghton Mifflin Company, 1926) pl. LXXX.
7. Marcus Whiffen, *American Architecture Since 1780*. (Cambridge, MA: M.I.T. Press, 1969) p. 75.
8. Philadelphia Inquirer, February 10, 1985.
9. Social Register, Philadelphia, 1904 (New York: Social Register Association, 1904).

8. Minor Ironwork Features

1. Marcus Whiffen and Frederick Koeper, *American Architecture, 1607-1976*. (London and Henley: Routledge and Kegan, Paul, 1981) p.255.
2. Pennsylvania Historic Resources Survey.
3. Leaflet published by the University City Historical Society.

9. Street, Park, and Garden Features

1. Margot Gayle and David W. Look, *A Historical Survey of Metals, in Metals in America's Historic Buildings*. (Washington: U.S. Department of the Interior, Heritage Conservation and Recreation Service, 1980) p. 71.
2. Samuel Sloan, *The Model Architect, an architectural pattern book*. (Philadelphia: E.S. Jones & Co., 1852. Dover reprint, 1980) Plate XXXVIII.
3. Frances Lichten, *Decorative Art of Victoria's Era*. (New York: Charles Scribner's Sons, 1950) p. 28.
4. Frances Lichten, ibid., p. 211.
5. Frances Lichten, ibid., p. 215.
6. Frances Lichten, ibid., p. 116.
7. Thomas Scharf and Thompson Westcott, *History of Philadelphia*. volume I, p. 686.
8. Page Talbott, *Philadelphia: Three Centuries of American Art*. (Philadelphia: Philadelphia Museum of Art) p. 330.

10. Good Ironwork Practice

1. Letter from Dallas C. Finch, Vice President, Marketing, Sherwin-Williams Company, March 1, 1999.

11. Unique Ironwork Solutions

1. "Art Nouveau" in Encyclopedia of Art. (New York: Greystone Press, 1968) p. 303.

GLOSSARY

acanthus: A thistle-like plant of the Mediterranean area. Its stylized leaves form the decoration of the Corinthian column capital. In scroll form, it often appears in the rinceau.

antefix: In Classic architecture, a decorated upright slab used to close the open end of a row of tiles. Usually decorated with the anthemion design.

anthemion: A Greek architectural ornament based on the flower of the honey-suckle or palmette.

architrave: The lower division of an entablature, the part which rests immediately on the capital of a column.

Art Deco: A decorative style associated with the 1925 Parisian "Exposition Internationale des ARTs DECOratifs et Industrieles Modernes." It is characterized by simplified curved and sharp angular or zigzag surface forms and ornaments. It was popular in the U.S. from the late 1920's through the 1930's.

Art Nouveau: A style of art, furnishings, and architecture characterized by ubiquitous use of undulation, like waves, or flames, or swaying flower stalks, or flowing long hair. It was popular at the turn of the 20th century.

Arts and Crafts: Starting as William Morris' English Neo-Medievalism, it was a style of furnishings, which spread to architecture. It emphasized handicrafts and, like Art Nouveau, was popular at the turn of the 20th century.

ashlar: Masonry made from stones which have been carefully cut so as to permit thin joints.

boot: Usually a casting, it is the heavy pipe extending up from an underground storm water drainage line to receive a downspout.

Byzantine Architecture: The style of architecture which developed in Byzantium, chiefly in the 5th and 6th centuries.

capital: The head or crowning feature of a column or pilaster.

Carpenters' Gothic: Part of the Gothic Revival movement which became popular in the mid-nineteenth century. The structures were built of wood, featured pointed arch openings, and were decorated with wooden filigree, popularly called "gingerbread."

cartouche: An ornamental tablet, often decorated and elaborately framed.

chamfer: To dull an edge by beveling off its right angle to a bevel of approximately 45-degrees.

Classical architecture: The architecture of Ancient Greece and Ancient Rome, and architecture using forms deriving from Ancient Greek and Ancient Roman architecture.

colonette, colonnette: A small column, frequently decorative.

Colonial Revival: An architectural style which first became popular at the turn of the 20th century. It incorporates forms and features found in the early architecture of the original thirteen colonies.

compression: A member is said to be in compression when the forces acting on it tend to cause it to shorten.

coping: The metal or masonry unit covering the top of a masonry wall.

Corinthian: See Order.

cornice: 1. The top unit of an entablature. 2. A continuous decorative element which projects from a wall at or near the roofline.

Doric: See Order.

entablature: The horizontal crown of a Classical order. Located above the column capital, it has three parts–the architrave, above that the frieze, and above that the cornice.

façade: The face of a building.

Federal: The architectural style of the early republic. It followed Colonial. It is characterized by its use of delicate Classical parts to articulate entrances.

foil: A clustered leaf-shaped ornamental form, combining a series of curved openings around a central point. The number of openings is indicated by a prefix, e.g. trefoil or quatrefoil.

frieze: The middle horizontal member of a Classical entablature, above the architrave and below the cornice. Friezes are frequently decorated.

gazebo: A garden pavilion. Gazebos are frequently located to command a good view.

Georgian Revival: Revival of an English architecture, that is Classical in its major exteriors. On the smaller domestic scale, it is far plainer. Georgian Revival was particularly popular early in the 20th century.

Gothic Revival: An architecture using forms mostly from medieval England and France. It became popular in the mid-nineteenth century as the Greek Revival declined. It was particularly favored for churches, rectories, and religiously oriented institutions.

Greek key: A geometrical ornament of repetitive horizontal and vertical straight lines, forming a band.

Greek Revival: An architectural style characterized by the free application of forms found in Classical Greek architecture. Popular in the early nineteenth century, its forms were made available principally from pattern books by Asher Benjamin and others.

Ionic: See Order.

Italianate: Straight fronted buildings, cubic blocks when free standing, frequently without any important projections excepting for their eaves. Roofs were virtually flat and were invisible from the street. Originating in England, in 1845, the style made its American debut in Philadelphia's Athenæum and in New York's long-razed A. T. Stewart Downtown Store.

Jacobean Revival: An architectural style using idioms from the architecture of Elizabeth I and James I of England. Characterized by its use of gables, decorative chimneys, and bays with grouped square-headed windows, it was particularly popular for suburban houses and college buildings.

lintel: A beam over an opening in a wall.

mansard: Named for the 17th century French architect Francois Mansart, it is a roof having two pitches, the lower one being steep and the upper one being relatively flat.

order: In Classical architecture, a column with base (usually), shaft, capital, and entablature, proportioned and decorated according to one of the accepted modes, the most common being Doric, Ionic, and Corinthian. The Greek Doric column has no base and its capital incorporates a compound curve profile. The Roman Doric column has a base, and its capital has a quarter circle profile. Both Greek and Roman Ionic columns have bases and their capitals include prominent large volutes. Corinthian columns have the most decorated bases and capitals, the latter incorporating small volutes and elaborate, stylized acanthus leaves.

pediment: The gable end of the roof of a Greek or Roman temple, or a feature resembling it in Classical architecture.

peristyle: A colonnade on all sides of a building or and interior court.

pilaster: 1. An engaged pier. 2. A non-supporting decorative feature simulating an engaged pier.

portico: A large porch with a roof supported by columns or pillars, often with a pediment.

quatrefoil: See Foil.

Queen Anne Style: The eclectic architecture of the late Victorian period, often combining medieval and Classical elements. The buildings are irregular in plan, massing and texture, frequently with gabled porches, round turret bays and decorative chimneys.

Richardson Romanesque: Popularized by the architectural genius Henry Hobson Richardson, this is a powerful round-arched style, usually wholly or partly of rock-faced masonry. Arches, lintels, and other structural features are sometimes of stones contrasting with the balance of the walls.

rinceau: An ornamental motif consisting of scrolls of foliage, usually of acanthus leaves.

rusticated: Masonry whose blocks have rough cut faces or beveled edges. Joints are conspicuous.

Second Empire: An eclectic architectural style popularized by the buildings of France's Second Empire, the empire of Napoleon III. Prevailing in the U. S. during the 1860s and 1870s, its most distinguishing characteristic is its use of mansard roofs.

tension: A member is said to be in tension when the forces acting on it tend to cause it to lengthen.

terneplate: A corrosive resistive coating applied over steel. It consists of an alloy of lead and tin.

terra cotta: A baked, usually hollow, molded clay building unit.

trefoil: See Foil.

treillage: Latticework.

Tuscan Villa Style: A mid-19th-century style of free-standing houses, usually large, composed of well defined rectilinear blocks, including towers, frequently off-center. Entrances are generally at the towers' bases. Roofs are low pitched and heavily bracketed.

Vitruvian scroll: A common motif in classical ornament, it is a series of scrolls connected by a wave-like band. Also called a running dog or a wave scroll.

volute: A spiral scroll, which appears most prominently in Ionic capitals and less prominently in Corinthian column capitals.

BIBLIOGRAPHY

Andrews, Jack. *Samuel Yellin, Metalworker*. Berlin, MD, 21811: Skipjack Press, Inc., 1992.

Andrews, Jack. New *Edge of the Anvil*. Ocean Pines, MD, 21811: Skipjack Press, Inc., 1994.

"Anvil's Ring," the Magazine of the Artist-Blacksmiths' Association of North America, PO Box 816, Farmington, GA, 30638.

Badger, Daniel D. *Badger's Illustrated Catalogue of Cast Iron Architecture*. New York, NY: 1865 Dover reprint, 1981.

Bannister, Turpin. "Bogardus Revisited." Journal of the Society of Architectural Historians, Philadelphia, PA: December, 1956 and March, 1957.

Burns, R.M., and Bradley, W.W. *Protective Coatings for Metals*. New York, NY: Reinhold Publishing Corporation, 1967.

Chiumenti, Ralph. "Cast Iron Architecture in Philadelphia." A pamphlet issued by the Old City Civic Association of Philadelphia, PA, and Friends of Cast Iron Architecture, New York, NY, 1976.

Davis, Myra Tolmach. *Sketches in Iron. Samuel Yellin, American Master of Wrought Iron. 1885-1940*. Washington, DC: Dimock Gallery, George Washington University, 1971.

Dilts, James D. and Black, Catherine F.; editors. *Baltimore's Cast-Iron Buildings and Architectural Ironwork*. Centreville, MD: Tidewater Publishing, 1991.

Feilden, Bernard M. *Conservation of Historic Buildings*. London: Butterworth Scientific, 1982.

Freedley, Edwin T. *Philadelphia and Its Manufacturers: A Handbook. Exhibiting the Development, Variety and Statistics of the Manufacturing Industry of Philadelphia in 1857*. Philadelphia, PA: Edward Young, 1858.

Gayle, Margot; Gillon, Edmund V., Jr. *Cast-Iron Architecture in New York: A Photographic Survey*. New York, NY: Dover Publications, Inc , 1974.

Gayle, Margot; Look, David W.; Waite, John G. *Metals in America's Historic Buildings: Uses and Preservation Treatments*. Washington, DC: U.S. Department of the Interior, National Park Service, Preservation Assistance Division, 1992.

Geerlings, Gerald K. *Wrought Iron in Architecture*. Charles Scribner's Sons, New York, NY, 1929. Reprinted by Dover Publications, Inc.; New York, NY, 1983.

Gerakaris, Dimitri; editor. "Samuel Yellin, Metalworker." The Anvil's Ring, summer, 1982.

Hawkins, William John III. *The Grand Era of Cast Iron Architecture in Portland*. Portland, OR: Binford & Mort, 1976.

Howell, J. Scott. "Architectural Cast Iron: Design and Restoration." The Journal of the Association for Preservation Technology, Vol.XIX, Number 3, pp. 51-55. 1987.

Jandl, H. Ward, editor. "The Technology of Historic American Buildings: Studies of the Materials, Craft Processes, and the Mechanization of Building Construction." Foundation for Preservation Technology, Association for Preservation Technology, P. O. Box 3511, Williamsburg,VA, 23187, 1983.

Jordy, William H. *American Buildings and Their Architects. Progressive and Academic Ideals at the Turn of the Twentieth Century*. Vol. 3. Garden City, NY: Doubleday & Co., 1972.

Lee, Antoinette Josephine, *The Rise of the Cast Iron District in Philadelphia*. Ph.D. dissertation. Washington, DC: George Washington University, 1975.

Lichten, Frances. *Decorative Art of Victoria's Era*. New York, NY: Charles Scribner's Sons, 1950.

Look, David W. *Inventory of Metal Building Component Catalogs in the Library of Congress*. Washington, DC: Department of the Interior, National Park Service, 1975.

Macfarlane's Castings. 6th edition. West Jordan, UT, 84088: Historical Arts & Casting, Inc.

Masson, Ann M. and Owen, Lydia J. *Cast Iron and the Crescent City*. New Orleans, LA: Gallier House, 1975.

"Metalworking: Yesterday and Tomorrow." New York, NY: American Machinist, 1977.

Mott, J. L. *Ironworks: Illustrated Catalog of Statuary, Fountains, Vases, Settees*. New York, NY, 1873.

Park, Sharon C. *The Use of Substitute Materials on Historic Building Exteriors. Preservation Brief No.16.* Washington, DC: Department of the Interior, National Park Service, Preservation Assistance Division, Technical Preservation Services, 1988.

Pierson, William H., Jr. *American Buildings and Their Architects. Technology and the Picturesque Garden City.* NY: Doubleday & Co., 1978.

Secretary of the Interior's Standards for Rehabilitation and Guidelines for Rehabilitating Historic Buildings. Revised edition. Washington, DC: Department of the Interior, National Park Service, Preservation Assistance Division.

Simpson, Bruce Liston. *Development of the Metal Castings Industry.* Chicago, IL: American Foundrymen's Assoc., 1948.

Sloan, Samuel. *The Model Architect, an architectural pattern book.* Philadelphia: E. S. Jones & Co, 1852. Dover reprint as Sloan's Victorian Buildings, 1980.

Southworth, Susan; and Southworth, Michael. *Ornamental Ironwork: An Illustrated Guide to its Design, History & Use in American Architecture.* Boston, MA, 1978: David R. Godine.

Sturges, W. Knight. *Introduction to the Origins of Cast Iron Architecture in America, including reprints of D. D. Badger's Illustrations of Iron Architecture and James Bogardus' Cast Iron Buildings.* New York: DaCapo Press, 1970.

Victorian Ironwork. A Catalogue by J. B. Wickersham, with a new historical introduction by Margot Gayle. Reprint of the J. B. Wickersham Catalogue of 1857. Athenaeum Library of Nineteenth Century America, Philadelphia, PA: Athenaeum of Philadelphia, 1977.

Waite, Diana S. *Ornamental Ironwork: Two Centuries of Craftsmanship in Albany and Troy.* New York. Albany, NY: Mount Ida Press, 1990.

Waite, Diana S. Editor and Introduction (American Historical Catalogue Collection) *Architectural Elements, The Technological Revolution.* Contains reprints of catalogs of iron: Marshall Lefferts & Bro.; Morris Tasker & Co.; Buffalo Eagle Iron Works; Keystone Mantel and Slate Works; Philadelphia Architectural Iron Co. Princeton, NJ: The Pyne Press, (undated).

Waite, John G., editor. *Iron Architecture in New York City: Two Studies in Industrial Archaeology.* The New York State Historic Trust in conjunction with the Society for Industrial Archaeology, Albany: NY, 1972.

Waite, John G. "The Maintenance and Repair of Architectural Cast Iron, with Historical Overview by Gayle, Margot." Washington, DC,: U.S. Department of the Interior, National Park Service, Cultural Resources, Preservation Assistance: Preservation Briefs, #27, 1991.

Wallace, Philip B. *Colonial Ironwork in Old Philadelphia: The Craftsmanship of the Early Days of the Republic.* Architectural Book Publishing Company, New York, NY, 1930: Reprinted by Bonanza Books Div. of Crown Publishers, Inc.

Walter, Thomas U.; and Smith, J. Jay. *A Guide to Workers in Metal and Stone.* Philadelphia, PA: Carey and Hart, 1846.

Wattenmaker, Richard J. *Samuel Yellin in Context.* Flint. MI: Flint Institute of Arts, 1985.

Waugh, Edward and Elizabeth: *The South Builds Chapel Hill.* University of North Carolina Press, 1960.

Wayne Iron Works. *Property Protection and Ornamentation.* A catalogue. Wayne Iron Works, Philadelphia, PA.

Weaver, Martin E. *Conserving Buildings.* New York, NY: John Wiley & Sons, Inc.

Webster, Richard J. *Philadelphia Preserved: Catalog of the Historic American Buildings Survey.* Philadelphia, PA: Temple University Press, 1976.

Whiffen, Marcus and Koepler, Frederick. *American Architecture: 1607 to 1976.* London and Henley, Ltd., U.K., Routledge and Kegan Paul, 1981.

Wickersham, J. B. *A New Phase in the Iron Manufacture. Important Inventions and Improvements; Historical Sketch of Iron; Descriptive Catalogue of the Manufactures of the New York Wire Railing Company.* Reprinted in 1977 by the Athenaeum of Philadelphia as *Victorian Ironwork: A Catalogue* by J. B. Wickersham with a new historical introduction by Margot Gayle.

Winthrop, Robert P. *Cast and Wrought. The Architectural Metalwork of Richmond, VA.* Richmond, VA: The Valentine Museum, 1980.

Wood, Robert; and Wood & Perot Catalogue. *A Catalogue of Iron Castings.* Philadelphia, PA: Robert Wood and Wood & Perot, 1853.

INDEX

SkipJack Books

Orders for SkipJack books, (available 24 hours a day) are processed by the fulfillment service BookMasters. All books and are shipped by UPS. Overseas shipping is handled on an individual basis. The current list of books is:

"Golden Age of Iron Work," Magaziner $39.00
      Hard cover, 224 pages, 2000

"Samuel Yellin, Metalworker," Andrews $19.95
      Paper back, 144 pages, 2000

"Colonial Wrought Iron," Plummer $44.00
      Hard cover, 256 pages, 1999

"New Edge of the Anvil," Andrews $25.00
      Paper back, 256 pages, 1996

"The Artist-Blacksmith's Craft," Schramm $29.00
      Includes the 24 page booklet, "Julius Schramm"
      Hard cover, 156 pages, 1987

Contact BookMasters by the following methods:
by calling   1-800-247-6553
by faxing   1-419-281-6883
or on the web   www.bookmasters.com/skipjack/

SkipJack Press
6 Laport Court
Ocean Pines, MD 21811

skipjack@ispchannel.com